INFLUENCING UP

INFLUENCING UP

ALLAN R. COHEN
DAVID L. BRADFORD

WILEY

John Wiley & Sons, Inc.

Published by John Wiley & Sons, Inc., Hoboken, New Jersey.
Published simultaneously in Canada.

For general information on our other products and services or for technical support, please contact our Customer Care Department within the United States at (800) 762-2974, outside the United States at (317) 572-3993 or fax (317) 572-4002.

Wiley publishes in a variety of print and electronic formats and by print-on-demand. Some material included with standard print versions of this book may not be included in e-books or in print-on-demand. If this book refers to media such as a CD or DVD that is not included in the version you purchased, you may download this material at http://booksupport.wiley.com. For more information about Wiley products, visit www .wiley.com.

Library of Congress Cataloging-in-Publication Data:

Cohen, Allan R.

  Influencing Up / Allan R Cohen, David L Bradford.
  Includes index.

  ISBN: 978-1-118-03845-1 (hardback)
  ISBN: 978-1-118-22223-2 (ebk)
  ISBN: 978-1-118-23609-3 (ebk)
  ISBN: 978-1-118-26091-3 (ebk)

    1. Influence (Psychology) 2. Persuasion (Psychology) 3. Interpersonal relations. 4. Business communication. I. Bradford, David L. II. Title.
  BF774
  658.4'09—dc23

                                                    2012001520

Printed in the United States of America

10 9 8 7 6 5 4 3 2 1

Contents

Preface

This began as a book about managing your boss. Although we had addressed this topic in *Influence without Authority*, we discovered that more and more organizational members were struggling with this issue. Some still complained about overcontrolling, micromanaging bosses who gave them far too little latitude, yet many others were concerned about distant bosses—often located far away—whose attention they could barely get and who seemed not to care about them. From dealing with "toxic witches" to "elusive withholders," many asked our advice about what to do. The writing for this edition was under way when our editor at John Wiley & Sons, Inc., Richard Narramore, asked us to consider the possibility of widening the scope of the book to deal with influencing other powerful, senior people, whether at the top of one's own organization or in another organization as potential customer or client, business partner, or vital stakeholder.

We soon saw that even in situations where the powerful person or group to be influenced was less accessible, our core concepts of reciprocity/exchange and treating the powerful as potential partners could ameliorate the negative impacts of great power differentials between the powerful and less powerful. Partnership might be tougher to implement when the powerful don't know you exist—or care to—but it is still a useful mind-set for transforming relationships. Power differentials harm both the powerful and the less powerful, yet influence always involves exchanging what the powerful care about in return for what is desired.

Furthermore, broadening the scope let us utilize what we know about making change from below, another increasingly important topic. Organizations have discovered that in a complex, competitive and changing world, initiative has to come from all levels in order to develop new products, services, and processes that can increase the top line after years of focus on cutting costs. But how do people below take initiative effectively?

At the same time, there has been a leap of interest and research about the behavior of the powerful when there are power gaps. Probably stimulated by the misbehavior of so many corporate and financial leaders, with the attendant parade of corporate and financial executives through the headlines or into court, researchers in many fields designed experiments, surveys, and fieldwork to examine the phenomenon. This was intriguing but somewhat one-sided in focus: seeing the behavior of only those with high power arouses great indignance but omits the role of the less powerful in perpetuating their perceived disempowered state. Seeing the interrelationships between those with high differences in power is a necessary part of the story. It is somewhat less satisfying because it reduces the ability to portray the powerful in totally negative ways—admittedly, occasionally totally deserved, as the victims of Bernie Madoff would attest—but includes the systemic effects collaborated with by the less powerful.

Most important, we concluded that the less powerful didn't have to wait for the powerful to magically be transformed into receptive supporters. They can use our concepts to influence even when those above aren't particularly welcoming or receptive.

The subject turned out to be incredibly intriguing. Although all influence is about exchange, it is extremely hard to make exchanges when the power gap is too large. This calls for reducing power gaps, not by reducing the power of those who have it, but by increasing the power of those who do not have enough. Making senior executives weak is not a very good strategy for growing healthy organizations. For powerful people to be really effective in the long run, they need to have powerful people below, even though many do not recognize this or even fight it. The blindness of the powerful that is a consequence of large power gaps often prevents them from seeing the benefits to them and the organization of having or helping strengthen strong players below.

Once we directed our attention to all this, we found many examples of people stuck on how to make a difference from below who could benefit from what we knew. We also found exciting examples of people who were achieving incredible gains, despite having little formal power. Thus we incorporated interviews, observations, reports by others, and numerous personal experiences where we can now stand back and draw useful lessons. We have included many of the inspiring (and instructive) examples in the book, but we had to leave some on the cutting room floor just to keep the book manageable length. We have added these additional examples to our website, www.influence withoutauthority.com.

Nevertheless, there is ample material in this book about how to gain influence to enable effective action by people who believe they don't have enough authority to command the results they want. Even high-power people can benefit from the analysis and examples we bring. Wherever you stand, we hope you will discover how to influence up.

Allan Cohen (Oakland, CA)
David Bradford (Berkeley, CA)

Acknowledgments

Many people have contributed greatly to the book, and we are deeply appreciative to all of them. Yet again we recognize that it takes an influential and caring village to make a book, and we tip our hats to every one.

Our editor, Richard Narramore, helped expand the application of our ideas and made many useful suggestions about the content. Christine Moore did a great job of helping us edit the manuscript into a viable length.

A large number of people provided rich and illuminating examples of the dilemmas involved in influencing upward, and often, how they managed to actually gain influence. Not all of the examples made it into the final edition of the book, due only to space restrictions, but all of them helped shape our thinking and refine our concepts. Thanks to Kathy Brown, Kristen Callahan, Jocelyn Cascio, Lisa Couture, Michael Cummings, Peter Dames, Johan DeBorst, Sam Doblie, Liam Fahey, Ruth Gilleran, Kate Granso, Rachel Greenberger, Paul Horn, James Hunt, Noel Johnson, JB Kassarjian (both for his stunning example in regards to access and great editorial suggestions), Nan Langowitz, Matt Larson, John Maraganore, Michael May, Mike McGuirk, Jennifer Morais, Joel Peterson, Dr. Bohdan Pomahac, Kelly Prescott, Lauren Simkin, Howard Simon, Tom Snow, Richard Snyder, Barbara Spangler, Kaoru and Naruhide Takashima, Karen Vrabel, Bob Weissman, and Yasuhiro Yamamoto.

We also want to mention the inspiration we have received from Nettie Seabrooks, whose entire career demonstrated how a person can be incredibly successful using exchange and dealing effectively with those who have power without ever resorting to self-aggrandizement or nasty tactics.

Iva Toudjarska went out of her way to introduce us to fascinating managers from whom we learned a lot. Bala Iyer was our tutor in the uses of social media, with help from Rachel Greenberger, giving us enough to cause our editor to wonder "how such old guys knew this stuff." Many of our students and managers who have attended our workshops also were very helpful through their questions, challenges, and suggestions.

Research assistant Dan Zolnierz unearthed useful material on power, while several people helped in various aspects of manuscript preparation: Mary Halpin, Wendy Glickenhouse, Kelly Hoover, Marlene Casciano, and Matthew McGuire. Without them, there could hardly be a manuscript!

We are especially grateful to Len Schlesinger, a person extremely savvy about power, both for the conceptual ideas he offered and the great examples from his own career. And as president of Babson, his support for working on the book was wonderful, as was the support of Provost Shahid Ansari and Dean of Faculty Carolyn Hotchkiss.

As always, the responses of our wives and kids provided not only support but instruction, and we are grateful.

PART

I

Fundamentals

1

The World Has Changed

To Be Successful You Need to Influence Up

Influence has always mattered at work. Whether it was necessary to obtain something—like a preferred assignment or a sale to an important customer—or minor favors like time off for personal events, it has always helped to have influence. Nowadays, having influence is even more important—because in order to move up in a company or impact other powerful organizations, you have to deal with a more challenging world.

The rapidity of change and uncertain economies has given way to more complex organizations that have a greater number of stakeholders whose cooperation is necessary—despite the simultaneous need for things to happen more quickly. Many people work in matrix organizations with multiple bosses, or they have jobs that cross departmental boundaries. This requires that they influence others who might not have the same goals or agree on what—or who—is necessary to succeed.

These days, you need powerful people to cooperate in terms of getting information, formal or informal approval to act, resources, introductions, and support (or room to maneuver) for implementation just to get your job done. Therefore, you can't achieve your objectives without getting help from others whom you do not control.

But merely doing your job won't guarantee that you'll advance. In an era of cost cutting and increased competition, organizations have to think about how to grow the top line and create new customers, products, markets, or processes that enable investment in growth. The employees who get ahead go beyond their job; they take initiative, create these opportunities, and solve problems that block progress.

This book is for you if you are trying to make significant contributions, yet are finding it increasingly difficult to do so because you need to influence people you can't control. It's usually not enough to point out impending problems/opportunities or even to propose solutions. You may have to garner support for your proposed solution or conduct small pilot tests. All of this involves the need to influence powerful people. Fortunately, you are likely in a position to have ideas that are of value to these powerful people. In fact, you are probably closer to the customer, and certainly to the operational problems, than more senior managers. You might have some special expertise or relevant past experiences.

As consultants, we frequently ask managers what they could do to make their organization a more creative, productive place, and the ideas tumble out. However, these are often quickly followed with a drop in enthusiasm as the manager sighs, "But there is nothing that I can do."

But there is plenty you can do, and we show you with scores of real examples throughout the book how others have found a way to overcome what at first appears to be a discouraging situation. We tell the story of Doug, a national sales manager of a multinational organization, who feels that he isn't able to use all his skills and knowledge because he has a micromanaging boss. There's Lucia Emerson at

"Grandetech," who is expected in her role as task force leader to figure out a new system that requires agreement from three very different divisions, each of which has its own objectives. There's also Peter Dames in the IT department at Toyota USA, who has to get on the radar of senior management so he can get them to accept new ways to use e-commerce. You might be like Indira Rai, who is doing well in a company she loves but is blocked from moving into a dream job by her possessive boss. Or you might be able to relate to a team of managers that has put together what they feel confident is an exciting new business idea and they need to gain senior management backing to go forward—even though their cobbled-together first product lost $6 million!

This book is not just for the employee who is expected to take initiative to produce change and bring in new ideas within a company. It's also for those who must influence customers, or for consultants who have to sell an ambitious game-changing project to a client who focuses only on cost—as Mike May from Accenture often did. Or perhaps your challenge is closer to that of Kristen Callahan, who is simply fighting to get an elusive, famous surgeon—the only one with a possible curative approach—to see her sick friend for a consultation. That's an influence success you will learn about in Chapter 12.

Most of the examples in the book describe actual situations, though we've altered specifics in some instances for privacy reasons. Only when we note that we are offering potential dialogue is anything *not* a report from our research and organizational observations.

The issues we discuss are increasingly being faced by managers at all levels, and they can present risks. Going directly to the chief executive officer (CEO), as Peter Dames did at Toyota, to demand that he come and see his department's demonstration is cheeky and could have the potential to be a career-limiting move. We don't deny that. However, "just doing your job," burying your head in the sand, avoiding anything that could possibly get you in trouble, and cursing your fate for having to deal with all those impossible people—these could be the riskiest behaviors of all! Although it is difficult, you need to find ways to successfully fulfill your current role while functioning like an entrepreneurial leader by constantly finding new and better ways to do things—and gaining the support you need to implement them.

This book is about how to both do your present job more successfully *and* take the initiative that will make you a more valued organization member. We can't totally eradicate risk, nor can we guarantee success; we can only put the odds in your favor by compelling you to see your relationships with powerful people in a different way. We provide knowledge about power differentials and how to overcome the obstacles, and encouragement to change some aspects of the way you have been operating.

Although there's no doubt that external realities such as very difficult bosses or remote senior managers can present significant challenges (problems we address in later chapters), we've found that you, the person seeking influence, often erect your own barriers to achieving that influence. The reasons for this are various and include the following:

- The assumptions you hold about how hard to push
- An unwillingness to raise a tough issue or have a difficult conversation with your boss
- A combative tone that provokes the exact reactions you dislike
- Fear of being turned down
- Inability to let go of your own concerns long enough to remember to give something valuable to get cooperation
- Any problems you might have dealing with authority

These self-limiting attitudes and behaviors are why you will have to take a tough look at yourself at various points in the book, while also carefully analyzing the person or group you need to influence. You have more ability to make a difference than you may think. It will help you to accomplish your goal if you keep in mind the following two conceptual themes that we present in this book:

1. Understanding the dynamics of power and overcoming the negative consequences of large power gaps.

2. Becoming a partner with high-powered people, whether as near as your boss, or as distant as a senior executive far up in your organization or in another organization.

Influence is exerted by reciprocity and exchange; in other words, people can be influenced when they receive something that they value in return for their response. Therefore, anyone can influence anyone else if they have something valuable to trade and can be trusted to deliver it. It's not always easy to figure out what people value, how to approach them, how to maintain trust, and how to make it clear that you aren't just looking out for your own interests. We built a generic model for working through all aspects of how to influence through exchange in our previous book, *Influence without Authority*. This book significantly expands on that model by providing examples of how to effectively apply influence when dealing upward.

The Impact of Large Power Differentials

In today's complex organizational world, you will increasingly be dealing with people who may be neither peers nor friends. These individuals have much more formal power than you have—and that's especially true when there are many organizational levels between you and those you need to influence. Middle managers have to deal with senior executives more often than ever, and they may need to influence across organizational boundaries as well. Regardless of whether it's within your organization or between your organization and another, the greater the power differential, the more difficult influence becomes.

Unfortunately, this kind of large power gap tends to produce dysfunctional behavior for people on both sides of the equation. Relatively high-power people tend to overvalue their own contributions and undervalue others', whereas those with less authority tend to overestimate higher-level individuals' power and underestimate their own. This makes it hard for both to get what they need. Higher-ups don't get the information and support they need to complete complex work, whereas those with less power fail to gain the credibility they need to use all of their capacities. We will discuss how this peculiar dynamic works in Chapters 2 and 3 and give suggestions throughout the book on how to overcome it.

Despite these challenges, most people have potentially much greater power than they think they do—and can therefore contribute more than they think they can without diminishing those in high-power positions. We will show how to effectively reduce these kinds of power differences so you can deal with high-power people—especially senior executives—and not fall into the traps that large power gaps often set. As long as you don't inadvertently give away your power, are willing to do your homework, and act with reasonable courage, you can increase your influence with a variety of high-power people.

Underlying our analysis is the little-realized phenomenon that power is usually *not a fixed amount;* it doesn't work in a way that means the more I take, the less there is for you. Thus, increasing your ability to influence usually does not require that you take away others' power. Instead, power is a *variable*, with a total amount that can be low or high. As we will demonstrate, you can decrease the power gap without decreasing the higher party's power. And since significantly increasing your influence can actually add to the other person's power, the outcome is usually win-win.

Becoming a Partner

Once you've come to understand what's at work in the dynamics of power differences, your second job is to adopt the mind-set that you must "become a partner" with authority figures. Although this may sound paradoxical in light of the usual characteristics of a power gap, it is a style of interacting that can have major positive consequences.

Relationships *do* matter for success in organizations. No one can accomplish much working alone, and the nature of how people connect with one another has major repercussions both for the organization's performance and for each individual's access to information and resources. This access determines effectiveness, reputation, and potential for advancement.

As everyone who has ever worked knows, work relationships have the potential to be unsatisfying and ineffective. Either or both parties can feel angry, stifled, mystified, vulnerable, misguided, untrusted, or deeply frustrated. Negative relationships frequently become frozen, with neither person knowing how to improve the relationship. This often leads to both people engaging in negative behavior, thereby aggravating each other and creating an atmosphere in which conditions only worsen and each person constantly blames—and tries to change—the other. Consistently battling these kinds of conflicts ultimately leads to separation—by firing, quitting, transferring, or just ignoring each other.

These negative relationships, however, are not the only kind; work relationships also have the potential to be satisfying and productive. We will describe and advocate a different approach to developing relationships between parties of unequal power. Although this emphasizes the connection you have with your boss, it also includes most other powerful people. This requires that both senior and junior employees move toward a *partnership* in which both are concerned for the other, voice their interests and differences, and think win-win where possible. You can "join with" the boss instead of just "reporting to" the boss—and at least sometimes, you can partner with those who usually expect only transactions, if anything at all.

This was the situation that Mary Quinn faced. She didn't think she could continue working for the "nasty witch" (Fran McNaughton, the vice president [VP] of development in a large software company), who had been her supervisor for the past year. She wrote "May 15" on the white board in her office, which was the day she would receive her bonus check. After that she could resign.

Mary, a business applications specialist, was based in New York, while Fran worked in the Boston office. Most of the time the two women spoke by phone, via abrupt and unpleasant conversations that Mary found dreadful. Fran's clipped, critical style and snapped-off orders had led Mary to feel that she was dealing with a corporate bully. According to Mary's description:

Fran had obviously never heard the maxim, "praise in public and criticize in private." I would suggest something and receive no response. Two minutes later another direct report would say the same thing and receive high praise. Fran ignored me at national conferences, and instead would hang out with the three tech guys on staff—people from whom I would hear that "Fran can't stand you." Though she heard good things about me, she clearly disliked me.

Although Mary's impulses were to demonize Fran and accept the status quo, or quit, she finally decided to take one shot at confronting her in person. She went to New York for a heart-to-heart talk:

Fran explained what aggravated her: "You go off and call meetings without me being aware; you do other things without asking, like take features out of an upcoming release to make the date without asking me." I acknowledged that what she said was true, but not meant to be disrespectful. I had just been trying to do the job as I had done it before . . .

She smiled for the first time during that conversation, and turned from an ogre into a nice human being. Suddenly we were both people meeting face-to-face, not just managers in a Corporation. Her demeanor changed, and she explained: "It's just that I hear after the fact . . ." I agreed, empathized, and told her how much I respected her knowledge—and her smile grew. I realized that we had both been running away from conflict up until that point.

I began to see her as someone who was trying to please her demanding management; she did have people screaming at her to "get it done yesterday." I therefore became much more sympathetic and invited her to my next meeting . . . I respected her expertise; however, it was hard to forget two years of bullying. So while we were not exactly friendly, we were no longer hostile.

(You can read about Mary and Fran in more detail at our website, influencewithoutauthority.com). What is so hard about directly talking to your boss about how he or she treats you? It seems like an obvious approach, yet way too many people are unwilling or unable to do it. Speaking directly to your boss about the relationship is not always easy to do, but it is a potent way of approaching a relatively powerful person with whom you need to have a productive relationship. Does it always work? Of course not. Your boss may be—at least in your view—far more miserable than Fran turned out to be—nastier, less willing to give credit, more of a micromanager, fearful of conflict. The best you can do in some situations is cut your losses, look for a way out as soon as possible, and resolve to learn from seeing the terrible effects that a really bad boss can have. The problem is that you might be as convinced of the futility of addressing the problem as Mary was. This attitude might be a result of your professional history, strong feelings, vulnerability and fear of being fired or losing the relationship—or just your lack of skill at working on a relationship.

So although it might have been true that Fran really "didn't like Mary" very much, and found Mary threatening and hard to control, she wasn't necessarily a bad person who enjoyed attacking at every opportunity. She was simply trying to meet the demands of her own superiors.

When you are in a relationship that has deteriorated like this, it is hard not to attribute all the blame to the boss's defects, or to assume that things will go badly if you try to address the problems in the relationship. Once you have decided upon your own explanation for your boss's (or any other person's) drawbacks, everything that happens tends to confirm your beliefs. Furthermore, since the boss *does* have the potential to affect your future, it can seem overwhelmingly threatening to open discussion on the subject. What if the boss retaliates?

It's hard not to begin to employ strategies like selective communication or even sheer avoidance as ways of manipulating the boss into not being too harmful. However, this book maintains that you want to influence your boss in a way that more closely resembles a partnership—admittedly with you in the junior partner role—in which each of you delivers in a more satisfying way. We will show you how to go about doing that—even in very difficult circumstances.

These two themes—understanding power differentials and partnering to enhance influence—are interrelated. People often consider power and relationships to be antithetical; they wonder, "Do I use all my power and ability to coercively push for what I want and risk alienating others, or do I go along for the sake of maintaining the relationship?"

However, these two themes are not only compatible; they in fact build on each other. The influence approach we use recommends that people actually build relationships; there is reciprocity and mutuality despite inequality of power, and taking a "partner" orientation increases your influence. Making powerful people partners helps determine their response to the approach. Because this partnering approach is founded on concern for mutual and organizational success, the assumption of potential partnership is most likely to gain cooperation.

Furthermore, understanding the power dynamics between these two groups can help you determine what matters most to those with higher power—which helps you figure out which approach to use to make influence success more likely. If you can accurately diagnose what powerful people value, you can determine how to persuade them and figure out what they might desire in exchange for what you want. It can also help you diminish the power differentials that prevent collaboration.

Example of Successful Upward Influence for Major Accomplishments

The following is the story of three colleagues who had to influence senior managers around a new, ambiguous, and uncertain opportunity after making an early blunder. Although managers involved in the project have insisted that the mistake remain confidential, it can be said that the scenario occurred at a well-known Fortune 100 industrial company that prided itself on incremental innovation. The three individuals manage different functions within a business unit at the company. However, the organization faced problems when one of their big customers complained that they weren't able to solve a recurring problem. The managers wanted to make everything right and believed that this customer provided an incredible market opportunity—if they could develop a product that used knowledge and resources from areas throughout the organization. They worked together with their boss's support, but kept his role behind the scenes because they were negotiating with the customer. They set about to cobble together a new piece of equipment that, if successful, could open up a whole new area of business.

It wouldn't have been possible in certain companies to get three separate functions with differing components to work together. Although it wasn't easy in this instance, this organization's boundaries were less impermeable, and the three individuals knew each other well. They collaborated to bring large components to one site, even renting a plane to fly in a piece from Europe. They successfully proved that all the parts could be assembled to work together, satisfying the large customer and completing a very large sale. The customer was billed, paid, and the deal was officially in the books.

However, accounting/finance was doing a year-end audit some months later and discovered that there was a $6 million cash loss on the sale. The managers had drawn bits and pieces and manpower from all parts of the organization that they hadn't formally tracked. This wasn't exactly the instant moneymaker they had thought it would be, and they hesitated, knowing that an unanticipated loss of that magnitude could be a career-stopper.

Nevertheless, the three men believed deeply that the product could be very successful if the company were willing to invest in it. They also knew that their competitors were probably working

(continued)

(continued)

on other solutions, so they tried to garner some support. They couldn't get the expense capitalized after the fact, and it was clear that they didn't have a promising business prospect if they couldn't find a way to dramatically reduce the costs involved in manufacturing the complete product. But they still believed in the opportunity. How could they not only gain forgiveness for creating a huge loss but also get to continue work on the product?

They had originally made a strong business case to their boss, and realized now that this might be the only way to recover the cash they had spent. He therefore supported their approach to a sector executive VP several levels higher. They knew this man only from Business Unit quarterly presentations, but thought he might be interested in nurturing a new venture as part of his charge, which included finding significant new sources of revenue. They argued their case that this was a way to help the company build a completely new breakthrough business. Their projections depended on what competitors would do, and they feared that competitors would solve the problem first unless they continued to refine the product. They had to figure out how to more than halve the cost of the product, and wanted a chance to work on it.

In turn, they offered an exchange: they would unofficially report and where necessary defer to him on every question, internal or external, about the first product, customers, technology, capacity, and so on. In return, they would inform him weekly or as often as he wanted about every aspect of what they were doing. That way, there would be no surprises, and he could pull the plug if they weren't making good progress. In effect, they were willing to provide ongoing reports to this executive VP while doing their own jobs, a kind of informal dotted line reporting relationship: a partnership. After intensive questioning, he agreed to provide "cloud cover" for them. It took a year, but they went on to build a very profitable business, currently reaping sales of more than $700 million a year.

Of course, not all attempts are so successful, especially if they so dramatically overspend in the first go-around. And even if they receive support from above, few would be able to gain the time to prove themselves; many more cannot even get past the reluctant, skeptical, or uncertain top management in the first place—either because a layered hierarchical organization inhibits their access, or because they don't present their proposal well. We will have a lot to say about how to be more influential; for now, take heart. If they could pull this off, you too can acquire major influence.

The Book's Organization

This book is divided into three parts:

- Part I, "Fundamentals," examines the dynamics of power (Chapters 2 and 3), then looks at our influence model (the Cohen-Bradford Influence Model; Chapter 4) and its application to an unhappy relationship between a national sales manager and the boss thought to be too controlling (Chapter 5).
- Part II, "Building a Powerful Partnership with Your Boss," examines in detail the challenges of building a partnership relationship with your boss. Chapter 6 expands the meaning of "true partner." Chapter 7 lays out the steps involved; however, this doesn't always go easily. Chapter 8 explores some of the common difficulties and how to overcome them. Chapter 9 extends the concept of partnership to describe various ways you can help your boss succeed (since that is what junior partners should do).

Part III, "Influencing Powerful People" (Chapters 10 to 15), looks at how to effectively deal with more distant senior executives. Power discrepancies come more strongly into play when interacting with these individuals. We will also look at the special dynamics involved when dealing with them from outside the organization. Although a "partner orientation" can still be helpful in dealing up many levels, it is less likely that you can generate the kind of tight relationship that is more possible with your direct boss.

When producing major change, you are probably going to have to influence multiple actors. To help you with this, Chapter 10 examines the process of identifying the relevant stakeholders and assessing their role in the change process. Because influence depends on knowing what is important to the other, Chapter 11 goes deep into how to assess powerful stakeholders' goals, needs, and concerns. It can be difficult to even gain access to powerful people far up the hierarchy, so Chapter 12 will lay out a variety of approaches. Chapter 13 looks at the actual give-and-take influence process that happens once face-to-face contact has been established.

Finally, we conclude with two chapters that provide major examples of how determined, persistent, and effective influencers have each used variations of what we've explained. Sometimes they've done so through careful diagnosis and plans; at others, by intuitively tuning in to the needs and concern of those whose cooperation they needed.

As suggested, we'll also introduce you to a number of other people who discovered that the challenging and (they assumed) "impossible" people they needed to influence were not necessarily lost causes. Their stories teach useful lessons and show how to apply the ideas we underline. We'll also provide some examples of influence failures, at least one of which led to expensive delays that cost one biopharma company millions because key stakeholders in a critical process were overlooked.

Think hard about whether all this is for you. If the risk is too high for you to bear—or if taking action could too easily lead to a career-limiting move—then you likely have to find a way to tolerate your status quo, or get out. However, we urge you to, at the very least, carefully analyze the possibilities before you give up. We deeply believe that you can be even more highly influential and effective.

Good luck!

CHAPTER

2

How Power Differentials Blind Smart People

Introduction

Have you ever found yourself furious at a person or group below you in your organization, wondering, "Don't they understand anything about what we do? Why do they look inward and fail to pay attention to our customers or industry conditions?" Do you begin your interactions with these people by assuming that they just don't have anything valuable to contribute, or haven't thought through their request? Do you put them down when talking to colleagues? Chances are, if you are like most people, you'd answer yes to at least some of these questions. Even the nicest people with the best intentions, when in a position of power, will give short shrift to people below them.

Or maybe you have been part of a group that feels manipulated; perhaps you've been asked to make recommendations, then you find that your suggestions are essentially ignored. Have you been furious but scared to confront the inauthentic manager who talks one way but acts quite another? Was this fear one of the reasons that caused you to stay silent?

It is remarkable how perfectly caring and smart people can be dramatically affected when they are on either side of a relationship in which a substantial power differential exists. This chapter and the next will show how these dynamics work, how both relatively high-power people and relatively low-power people impact each other in ways that can impair both parties—including the apparent winners on the higher end of the power scale. We will help you figure out what tactics to use to influence anyone more powerful than you.

It isn't news that great discrepancies in power can cause great problems for both ends of the spectrum. As Thomas Jefferson pointed out, "Power believes it has a great soul and vast views, beyond the comprehension of the weak, and that it does God's work while it violates all his laws." In other words, the powerful come to believe that they are doing something inherently right, and overestimate their own competence; they assume that they're allowed to break the rules. The less powerful, on the other hand, underestimate their capacity to be heard without punishment—and in the process lose a considerable amount of effectiveness.

"The Emperor's New Clothes," a Hans Christian Andersen story based on a fourteenth-century Spanish tale, is a good illustration of how the dynamics of power work. The story suggests that the illusions, or at least the pretensions, of the powerful can be seen by the less powerful, but it takes a child too young to understand the expectation of keeping quiet in the presence of such a high-power person to speak up and point out the emperor's nakedness. Many interpretations of this tale have been made, but the behavior differential between high- and low-powered people is familiar across many cultures.

This doesn't mean that power in itself is the problem. On the contrary, power is necessary for organizational success because it is the driving force required to get things done. Don't you want a boss who has the power to get resources, grant permission, and open doors? And don't you want power yourself to do your job and achieve goals above and beyond expectations? The negatives arise when a large power gap exists between people or groups—along with the blindness and silence such gaps tend to create.

Common Negative Consequences of Having Relatively Great Power

The destructive impact of large power discrepancy was shown in the classic "prison experiment" conducted by Philip Zimbardo at Stanford University in 1971. In the experiment, people randomly chosen to play prison guards rapidly degenerated to abusive behavior. Power simulations by Oshry and by Bolman and Deal had similar results—people who were assigned arbitrarily to high-, middle-, and low-power groups began to behave accordingly remarkably quickly. These findings show how much behavior is shaped by relative degree of power rather than by individual predisposition.[1]

Bolman and Deal's simple classroom simulation arbitrarily divides participants into three groups. Ground rules dictate that a high-power group decides assignments and allocates resources, and a low-power group has to wait for instruction that a middle-power group conveys between levels. We have used this model with executives, MBAs, and undergraduates; in every population, the high-power group (often trying to be fair and reasonable) gets wrapped up in discussions among themselves, whereas the low-power group fumes about being restricted and waits impatiently to hear from the top. In less than an hour, even very individualistic, antiunion managers in the low-power group begin to rebel; they threaten to organize like a union, refuse to complete assignments, and lose patience with the top group. A few try to curry favor with upper management by acting as trusted helpers; however, most quickly gravitate toward collective action, which can increase their voice and impact, or go passive.

Meanwhile, the top begins to look down on and discount or patron-ize what they might call "those short-sighted workers," becoming trapped in its own deliberations. (As in many organizations, those in the middle are truly caught there; they begin to lose respect from both the high- and low-power groups). We see here a perfect example of the dictum that *situation shapes behavior*—and situations with great power discrepancies shape negative responses at both extremes.

This pattern is demonstrated repeatedly in research and in our own experience: Relatively powerful people tend to *overestimate* their own contributions and intelligence, and *underestimate* the con-tributions and intelligence of lower-power people. In turn, relatively low-power people tend to *overestimate* the power of and likelihood of retribution from high-power people, and *underestimate* their own actual and potential power to shape behavior.

Several factors[2] contribute to and reinforce this negative pattern. Higher power entities:

- *Spend more time with elite people and groups*, leading them to dehu-manize and stereotype lower-power people.[3]

- *Are more oblivious to what other people think*. This reduces their awareness of the way they are perceived by others, and makes them less able to accurately interpret what people around them are saying and more likely to pursue their own desires. It also makes them verbally dominant, making more assertions instead of exploring options. These attributes lead them to become more confident, more inclined to express their true attitudes, not care as much about what others think and say,[4] "and jump in to argu-ments,[5] . . . with less changeable attitudes,"[6,7] which reduces their notion of how much attention to pay to others.

- Furthermore, they *believe that they are more perceptive* and have personal control, overestimating the areas in which they have expertise and underestimating dangers even in areas over which they have no power.[8] In turn, they are more responsive to organizational goals than to feelings.[9]

- As a result, they believe that rules are made to be broken[10] so *are more likely to violate ethical standards while believing that they are more honest* (therefore they come off as hypocritical),[11] and are actually more comfortable with lying so are better liars.[12]

- Often *believe they have to hide their vulnerability*, for fear that making it visible will diminish their power, even though the opposite can often turn out to be true.

- Similar dynamics also operate within teams, where *high-power leaders often discount and diminish the views of most team members.*[13]

It would be hard to find a more vivid example of what can happen as the power gap grows than the saga of Jeff Kindler, chief executive officer (CEO) at the giant pharmaceutical company Pfizer. Kindler was a former litigator whose intelligence, toughness, sponsorship wins, and political maneuvering led him to the top. *Fortune* magazine used exhaustive investigation to discover that Kindler was fired in December 2010 for behavior marked by domination and intimidation through micromanaging and second-guessing or berating executives—even bringing many to tears. He also dismissed both executives and scientists with deep expertise, showed favoritism to a controversial head of human resources who eventually had to be fired by the board, shouted at a board member at a retirement party, and delayed—then frequently reversed—critical decisions.

Although Kindler acted for some time in a manner that allowed him to get his way, his attitude also planted the seeds of his own destruction. High-power people tend to forget about how much they need those below them as they increasingly discount others' worth—thereby hindering performance.

Here are some examples of quotations that show a powerful person who got too powerful relative to almost all those below him:

"Jeff seemed to believe he was the only smart guy in the room . . ."

"Kindler . . . bombarded [his deputies] with . . . questions at all hours . . . regularly scheduled conference calls on weekends . . . seemed oblivious to executive vacations . . . [and] expected immediate responses to his questions . . .”

All that did not only make life miserable for Kindler's team; it also clogged the company's decision-making process. Kindler was a voracious consumer of information—often a strength but increasingly a weakness.[14] He bombarded his staff with ideas or questions during the night, and they would have to divide the assignments just to cope, whether or not they were worth exploring.

The Necessity of Power—But "Mind the Gap!"

None of this is to suggest that Kindler didn't have good ideas or wasn't willing to take on needed cost-cutting, reorganization, and strategic redirection. It also shouldn't diminish the importance of power and power differentials in accomplishing organizational goals. After all, power in the social/organizational realm is the ability to get others to behave in ways they might not otherwise choose— and sometimes that is necessary for organizational transformation, growth, or survival. Power differentials also help to preserve order, by ensuring the appropriate division of labor that allows the various units and individuals to fulfill their distinct roles. Those who know of the need for change can mobilize others while overcoming inertia and resistance. Without legitimate power differentials, it would be very hard for any organization of more than 10 or so to make decisions and to move forward.

The problem is therefore not with inevitable and desirable power, or even with power differentials. Problems come into play when the gap between the powerful and the less powerful is too large. At first blush, this gap might seem like a good thing; powerful people can accomplish things without (visible) opposition. But that assumption is extremely short-sighted, because a large power gap hurts those with very high power as well as those with very low power. There are two important reasons why the gap harms both high-power and low-power people:

1. **High-power leaders need powerful members.** High power might *command* obedience, but it does not guarantee commitment, initiative, or excellence. Leaders need influential people to carry out orders and directions, to provide knowledge, and often to be the sources of specialized input and creativity that lead to improved ideas, opportunities, and achievements.

2. **High-power leaders need the check that empowered members can provide.** Most of the negative consequences described above are due to the lack of appropriate resistance. Questioning an impulsive or uninformed decision does not have to be equated with disloyalty or insubordination; these questions can be the ultimate form of support.

Even though some people end up abusing their power, it is not much help to either them or their organizations to strip away everyone's power. Low-power leaders who are unable to get things done do not generate enthusiasm, gain followers, or create organizational growth. This kind of collective weakness and apathy can cast a pall over everything.

The solution is to create more *combined power* between higher- and lower-power people. This doesn't reduce a higher-up's power; it simply increases that of the less powerful, and leads to an overall net increase of power—and therefore to an overall increase in the capacity to *make things happen.* For those below, effectively exercising power means helping others accomplish valued objectives. For those above, using power to enhance others' power actually creates more total power. Ironically, when higher-ups are willing to create more power for those less powerful than they are, the lowers will in turn want to grant power above—because the actions of the higher-ups have increased their feeling that it is possible to influence up.

Power that is not invested in goals beyond one's personal ambition—power that is not, in other words, *socialized power,* as the psychologist David McClelland[15] has called it—is thus power wasted. Although smart investments increase power, overuse diminishes it. Invested power yields positive returns; however, if it forces people to do things they do not value, it eventually diminishes them. Similarly, those who abuse their positions of influence will diminish their power, as it often prompts resentment or fear that inhibits future cooperation. Resentful and dependent lower-power people often subtly sabotage by passing responsibility upward and creating more burdens. For these reasons, effective executives prefer to use influence, and not coercion, whenever possible—even with those to whom they can legitimately give orders.

This is not to deny that there are some situations where power *is* a fixed amount ("so the more that I have, the less that is available to you"). That is the situation in many negotiations, for example. Also, even smart people with differing responsibilities can disagree on how to proceed. And there are times when programs have to be cut, operations closed down, people terminated, when it is impossible or impractical to attain consensus. Therefore, coercion is sometimes necessary to achieve important goals. Unwillingness to persuade others when it's appropriate or necessary actually diminishes one's power. This way of using power often arises when the various parties have incompatible goals. However, in dealing with one's boss or influencing those higher up the power scale, there are many more times when goal alignment is possible, and allows for using influence as described in this book.

Sources of Power—Organizational and Personal

When addressing power gaps, it helps to understand that power comes from access to information, resources, and relationships. These things enable power. They can come as a result of formal organizational position that assigns access, and/or from personal qualities that induce others to be willing to follow. People can enhance their personal power with positional power, or they can be influential without positional power. For example, Jeff Kindler's roles at Pfizer—general counsel, vice chairman, and CEO—gave him access to detailed knowledge about the business, important people such as board members and senior executives, and huge budgets. In addition, his brilliant, forceful personality (and apparently charm) prompted many people to willingly follow him. Kindler's intensity—which some viewed as intimidation—was labeled by others to be drive and vision. The Fortune article points out:

> [A former CFO] . . . and others say they view what some, in Pfizer's nonconfrontational culture, saw as anger instead as passion or intensity. (They say that same intensity helped Kindler play a key role in persuading Big Pharma to back President Obama's health care plan.)

Power is always relative; almost no one has *zero* power in a given situation. Those lower in the organization also have access to at least some information, resources, and relationships. On a national scale, one of the more dramatic historical examples of success from below was that orchestrated by Gandhi: unarmed citizens were able to stand up to armed British troops and eventually win. The world has recently seen instances in several extremely hierarchical Middle Eastern countries where peaceful demonstrators have been able to overturn dictators through collective action.

Focusing on relative power compels us to think about the interaction between the relatively powerful and the relatively powerless. It doesn't matter where the behavior starts; once high-power people act in a dominant way, that can cause lower-power people to reinforce the behavior. The opposite is also true; a relatively low-power group's passivity can cause the relatively powerful to behave in dismissive ways that only reinforce the passivity. But just blaming one group discounts the dynamic interactivity between the groups. Each triggers undesirable behavior in the other, so the actions of both groups need to be considered.

Bad Patterns, Not Bad People

When the behavioral consequences of power are considered, it's easy for either group to write off the other. The lower-powered might say, "I can't stand those arrogant, smug SOBs," and the higher-ups might say, "Why can't those wimps speak up or have an original thought about what's good for the organization?" If you are like many people thinking about how to influence higher-power people, you might someday be in the flipside situation, in which you are the one looking down your nose from above. No matter which group you find yourself in, you should try to resist seeking a way to feel superior to the group with which you do not identify. Instead, try to better understand how you can overcome the costs of a large power differential.

The negative effects of the power differential are rarely intentional, and only a few can be blamed on high-powered individuals' personalities. Although there are people who are inclined to dismiss just about everyone—and some who are intimidated by most people they encounter—either affliction reduces the likelihood of filling and holding responsible organizational positions for long. Even though those at the top are frequently determined and competitive, the usual pressures of occupying a high-power position more often drive the dismissive behavior, which, in turn, contributes to what makes upward influence difficult. *Not everyone with high relative power succumbs to the pressures*, but it helps to understand both the probability that they will and the methods for overcoming the consequences. We've observed that the negative patterns usually result from *differences in the perspectives* between high- and low-power people. Whether it's due entirely to the fact that these individuals have been in positions to acquire power—or whether it just came as a result of their personalities—people who reach upper organizational levels must focus on broader issues, external forces, and organizational direction. They are expected to "think strategically." On the other hand, those in lower-power roles tend to concentrate on fulfilling immediate tasks and conditions—to "meet their objectives."

When people at the top spend a large portion of their time planning for issues that get far less attention from those below, they naturally believe that it is their (wonderful) personal characteristics and capacities that allow them to "see more and farther." They don't realize how much time they have been working on—often even obsessing about—complex and challenging issues. Even when they have tried to convey this information to others, many people don't absorb it.

These failed attempts to communicate are therefore likely to make people worry about impending danger, or assume that they need to change course. This leads almost everyone to eventually perceive a deficiency in the system—which in turn inhibits the chance that higher-ups will listen to the opinions or views from people below. Eventually, less-powerful people assume that higher-ups simply won't listen to them. Of course, because many people hold ingrained negative beliefs, learned through experience, about what it means to deal with people at the opposite end of the power spectrum, it often doesn't take much to "confirm" their negative expectations of the other tribe. Once you decide that the other side is intimidating and uninterested, or short-sighted and feeble-voiced, it is hard to notice any evidence to the contrary.

Do some people in elevated positions become power-hungry? Are they so focused on acquiring power that it becomes an end in itself? Unfortunately, the answer is yes. Even more unfortunately, there are some hard-nosed "experts" who claim that acquiring personal power is more important than doing something valuable with that power. Some people will urge you to become totally Machiavellian and seek power for its own sake. From these people you will hear advice such as, *Don't be afraid to bully, intimidate, or use fear if you want to keep your power; you get an advantage from appearing a little tough or even mean* or *Forget about being honest and self-disclosing; others will use that against you.* They'll also tell you: *Don't be put off by old wives' tales about bad things happening to people who desperately want to get ahead; good things happen to powerful people.*

Joel Peterson, chairman of the board of JetBlue and former CEO of the real estate development company Trammell Crow, argues the opposite. Peterson maintains that power comes from competence, not from bullying, and that managerial mind-set works best when it isn't "all about me," but rather focused on achieving common goals.

We agree with Peterson. This doesn't mean that it isn't necessary to have to occasionally "play hardball"; however, you should play this way only as the last resort, and you can play fairly. In fact, those who believe that it's all about enhancing their own power set up a self-fulfilling prophecy. If you constantly put yourself first without bothering to consider how your actions impact others, others will likely respond in kind—which further weakens trust all around.

Powerful people who operate with short-term, "me-first" thinking are wrong about what it takes to acquire and sustain power. Many have been temporarily successful but were blown out of the water when they persisted in trying to make themselves look good. Others have tried to climb the corporate ladder but froze on the way up due to the mistrust they created. Most contemporary organizations must bring together diverse experts to resolve complex problems, and require far too much collaboration for those playing only for themselves to succeed.

We don't have to demonize powerful people. By assessing the dynamics of interactions between high-power and low-power people, we can keep from personalizing differences in views, and avoid blaming individuals or entire groups. However, few organizational members manage to shake off the tendencies that mutually reinforce beliefs in others' deficiencies. Certainly, some very powerful people are so determined to have their way that they don't see the long-term consequences of stepping on or diminishing others. Yet helping them notice may influence their behavior.

Consider Chandran Menon, the founder and CEO of Menon and Menon Diesel Engines in Kolhapur, India. A brilliant and dynamic entrepreneur, inventor, and self-taught engineer, Menon recognized that managing wasn't the same as creating a company, and he was determined to learn also to be an extraordinary manager. He decided to run an executive development retreat and hired one of us (Allan) and a young, inexperienced colleague named Mollie to facilitate.

Early in the workshop, small task groups went off to work on assignments. They returned, and the first group was barely two minutes into their report when Menon—who wanted to correct an assumption they'd made—burst in to tell them how wrong they were. His outburst resulted in complete silence. Mollie replied, "I wasn't particularly committed to this idea when we discussed it in our group. But you were so rude and insulting that now I want to defend the idea fiercely."

This stunned Menon into silence. After a few awkward moments, with welling tears, he confessed, "I had no idea. Will you please all forgive me?"

Menon later marked that moment in his official biography as a turning point in his own leadership evolution. It was the point at which he stopped allowing his brilliance and dynamism—the very brilliance and dynamism that had led to his disproportionate power—to inhibit others.[16] Although these realizations are not always so effective or immediate, this was a case where, like the child telling the emperor he had no clothes, one voice made a difference to a powerful person whose brilliance had gotten the better of him.

Influence challenges are not just a consequence of high-powered people's bad behavior; they result from the interaction between the higher-ups' actions and the lowers' action (or inaction). If Mollie hadn't said anything to Menon, it would have looked like he was arrogant and impervious to feedback from those below him—partially because he would have had no idea of his behavior's impact. He could have continued thinking, as often happens, "If they had anything to contribute they would have done it; their silence proves they have too little to offer."

This is why we'll now examine what it is that relatively low-power people do to compound the difficulties in interactions with higher-power people. And from there we will go on to provide plenty of advice about how to gain influence, even from the lower-power position.

CHAPTER

3

How Power Differentials Give Smart People Laryngitis

Despite all the research on what powerful people do, there has been much less about the impact on the less powerful, and especially on the consequences for the powerful of the reactions. Yet we believe that it is the systemic interactions that make a big difference in organizations.

If, as we've determined, too much power blinds people, too little tends to silence them or cause other, potentially self-defeating behavior. Furthermore, those who believe they have too little power often end up hurting those with more power—which in turn inhibits the entire organization. If you are going to be influential from a relatively low-power position (which is a lot better strategy than waiting to act for sudden enlightenment of the powerful!), you must understand this dynamic. Understanding the following three core concepts can help you avoid the disadvantages associated with a low-power position:

1. Power can be actual or virtual; if people *believe* someone has power, then they have it, because they will behave accordingly.
2. When faced with a large power gap, either party can cause a dysfunctional interaction—and either party can correct it.
3. Laryngitis among those below is damaging to those in high-power positions as well as to the ones in the low-power positions.

Let's look at each of these concepts in more detail, so that we can begin to show how to overcome the bad effects of large power differentials.

Actual versus Virtual Power

In Chapter 2 we discussed the bases of power—access to information, resources, and people—that give some people more clout than others. Occasionally, however, individuals obtain power for the sole reason that lower-level people hand it over to them. The mere *appearance* of being powerful can be enough to cause others to treat the apparently powerful as capable of forcing (or enforcing) behavior, whether or not that is truly the case. Power grows because everyone knows that people with actual power can either help them or punish them. So when people *believe* that someone has power, they won't test that belief—thereby making that person or group powerful without having to demonstrate it. The Wizard of Oz was quite powerful—even feared—until the curtain was pulled, revealing a little old man.

Lower-level people give away power in the following ways:

- **They believe and act on myths that exist in almost every company.** For example, Allan was one of the original Work Out consultants at General Electric, where he helped a team formed by the one business's vice president (VP) of research and development come up with an innovative organizational recommendation. But a team member who was a trusted lieutenant of the VP warned the team that they could not offer their idea: "You know that at GE you can't tell the truth, so we can't present this!" The VP had asked for the recommendation, and Work Out had been invented to encourage people below to speak up. However, this didn't matter at all.

- **They remember a historic incident—accurately or not—and take it as a lesson.** Allan challenged the lieutenant in the GE incident, who insisted, "I remember when 'Joe Fisher' stood up at a meeting and disagreed with the general manager in this division. He was gone a week later." Task force members fell silent. As it turned out, Joe had been underperforming for a long time, and his departure many years ago was totally coincidental. But the incident lived on, magnified in memory, and affected current employees' behavior.

- **They give inappropriate deference to authority.** This is such a potent phenomenon that it has even been documented to cost lives. For example, several studies revealed that some airline accidents were caused by copilots refraining from correcting pilots in error, because they did not feel comfortable correcting "a superior."

- **They misinterpret ambiguous signals.** A senior manager became aware of considerable anxiety in the ranks during a major organizational change, even though top management had guaranteed that there would be no layoffs. Hoping to relieve some of this concern, the senior manager told employees, "I visited [the other large company in the area] the other day, and their senior vice president told me, 'everybody around here is so worried about the economy that they think that they are all toast. Can you imagine them being so worried?'" Several days later, the senior manager discovered—to his horror—that the story he had intended to be a stress reducer had made some people even *more* anxious. It had also angered others who thought he was saying *they* were "toast."

- **They set up self-fulfilling prophecies.** This can take several forms. One is to offer up watered-down or indirect suggestions and, when the more powerful leap in with clarifications, ideas, directions, or orders, conclude that they had already made up their mind. A variation is to raise their concerns in question form, which the higher-power person takes at face value and responds "Yes, I have given it considerable thought." The timid questioner then concludes that the powerful one can't be influenced, rather than recognizing his role in inducing that person's response.

- **They fall into the trap of previous success.** We call this the *curse of the powerful*, because one of the ways the powerful have gained power is by being insightful. Therefore, it wouldn't make sense for them to stop making valuable contributions, but the more often they are on target, the greater the temptation for those below to go along even when they aren't certain. This can be costly because strong leaders need strong followers to oppose them when they are going astray. The problem is that the smarter high-power people are, the more readily lower-power people give in to them—even when they should resist.

For all these reasons, the lower-power person jumps to conclusions about powerful executives without bothering to check whether they are true. This reluctance can be based on fear of retaliation or on fear of making a career-limiting move (CLM), but can also be due to the perception that the victim role provides a degree of safety: "I would really speak up, but I am helpless because of those oppressive bosses."

When employees fear negative reactions—criticism, loss of privilege, even firing—they're simply too scared to even *test* taking a stand. No one is eager to make a CLM; if this seems even remotely possible, many people prefer to simply assume the worst. Many individuals live by "better safe than sorry" rather than "nothing ventured, nothing gained."

As two excellent researchers, Amy Edmonson and James Detert, argue:

> Fear of speaking up is over-determined by both [human nature] and the modern economy's specific realities. . . . We're

hard-wired to overestimate rather than underestimate certain types of risk—it was better (for survival) to "flee" . . . from threats that weren't really there than to *not* flee the one time there was a significant risk. So, we've inherited emotional and cognitive mechanisms that motivate us to avoid perceived risks . . .

[Most people today] depend on hierarchical organizations and their agents (i.e., bosses) to meet basic needs for economic support and human relationships. Thus, fear of offending those above us is both natural and widespread.[1]

Organizations everywhere have lower-power people who are afraid to offer, in a direct, impactful way, the relevant information or their unvarnished views of the situation. This kind of "laryngitis" does not serve the organization as a whole, nor does it benefit those in high-power positions or those below—everybody loses. People might be willing to speak up if they knew that there would be no retaliation even when the news was not welcome, but in the absence of certainty about what might happen, voices are muted. When is the last time you witnessed—or were part of—that kind of loss of voice? It happens so often that some people consider it inevitable, and give up hope that there can be genuine openness.

The Danger of a Dysfunctional Dance

The action of a high-power person moving in and taking over and the behavior of the low-power person holding back are interrelated in that each triggers the other. It doesn't matter who was the first mover. Was it the direct report who wasn't sufficiently thorough in the analysis or was it the manager who went over the report, yet again, with a fine-tooth comb? So the manager makes some corrections and additions. The employee doesn't think these are all that significant but (silently) concludes that "the boss has to show how smart he is," and next time the employee leaves out a few minor points so that the boss can contribute. The manager sees that the work is incomplete so examines the new report in even more detail and the escalation continues.

Of course, each party blames the other. "If I really had competent people, I wouldn't have to waste my time doing their job for them," says the boss. "My micromanaging manager takes away all the motivation to do the quality work I want to do" is the conclusion of the employee. This cycle confirms what high-power people tend to think already: that they shouldn't listen to or trust lower-power individuals and groups, and that they need to supervise them closely. It doesn't matter where in the organization the dysfunctional behavior originates; once the cycle begins, it perpetuates itself. Each side's behavior "confirms" to the other that their assumptions are correct—and that they should continue behaving as they have been.

Even though either party can start this dysfunctional dance, the good news is that either can also end it. This escalating cycle can only continue if it is not discussed. As we will show throughout the book, it is possible for the lower-power person to change the game, often by addressing the issue. We can offer no guarantees that pointing out the "dance" always works, but using the approaches that we will explore in subsequent chapters can significantly reduce the risk and increase the probability of success.

The Costs to Both Parties

In Chapter 2 we discussed the need of high-power people for those below to tell the truth. No matter how competent leaders are, they are bound to have ideas that don't work and can cause damage. It is a gift to be warned that driving the organization in the present direction might take it over a cliff or prevent seizing new opportunities. Furthermore, being surrounded by sycophants increases the danger that leaders start to believe their infallibility. Inspiring laryngitis in those below—who often are closer to the problems and opportunities—can be disastrous. It is best to be told when one is not wearing any clothes.

We also discussed that leaders need strong employees both to implement decisions and to take initiative on their own. In our previous work on leadership, we argued that excellence comes when full use is made of everybody's abilities, which doesn't occur when those below feel they are being ignored and not heard.

Another cost of a large power gap is that it forces the employee into a dependent role; but healthy individuals resist dependency. They tend to respond by (a) reducing the powerful party's power, (b) leaving the playing field, or (c) going passive (or passive-aggressive).

If (overt or covert) rebellion is too dangerous and it is not possible to leave, the highly dependent may go passive—or even more damaging—*passive-aggressive*. One way in which lower-power people may attempt to inhibit powerful people's sway is by sabotaging them. The classic approach is to "work to rules" by doing exactly—and *only*—what he or she has been instructed to do. This works because almost no high-powered person can imagine all the possible contingencies to any complex action. When the lower-power person follows directions in an inflexible way, a major problem is likely to arise, which can be met with, "but I did exactly what you said." Another form of sabotage is to withhold crucial information, "forgetting" to inform. Sabotage, of course, can be even more destructive. In the old days this could be something like dropping a handful of bolts into a panel while assembling a car, thus insuring a permanent rattle. Currently it can be done by programming a so-called Easter egg (nasty surprise) into software, by "leaking" private material on purpose, or even by going so far as to spread malicious rumors in an attempt to harm reputations.

Some low-power people do what amounts to basically retiring while still on the job. Today's fast changing world requires high member initiative for organizations to succeed. But everybody has probably had coworkers who just shuffle papers.

On the other hand, in the presence of powerful people and authority, a fraction of people feel compelled to test that power all the time. These people are generally perceived as a royal pain in the butt. Although their lack of fear of speaking up might be a positive attribute at times, they go too far, and powerful people usually avoid them—unless they win and become one of the more powerful themselves.

Finally, some people prefer to unite or become dependent on others. These are the organizational "yes men" who work very hard to get on powerful people's good side. This is easier, of course, if they happen to agree with the powerful people; but even if they don't, they will do their best to make it seem as though they do. One interesting study found that skill at concealing flattery was positively correlated with senior executives receiving appointments to other companies' boards; however, flattery that was perceived as *attempted* flattery did not work well at all.[2]

In general, low-power people have an incentive to make high-power people think that they support them. They assume that it is better not to get on their bad side.

Some, of course, get so fed up or so uncomfortable with the unexpressed feelings they accumulate that they put all their energy into getting transferred to another part of the organization where they think they will be treated better, or quit outright. These are people who won't even tell the truth about their disaffection in exit interviews ("you never know who this could get back to"), and if they do, it comes out sounding petty because they are so upset.

None of these coping styles helps the organization or the high-power person, and it certainly does no good for those with little power. It prevents truth from being told, real issues from being raised, and those below from showing and growing their competence.

Conditions for Altering Power Relationships and Narrowing the Gap

The rest of this book will address the various ways to overcome the barriers to influencing powerful people. First we want to provide a brief overview of the dimensions of the process.

The first step is to start with yourself. Unfortunately, the cartoon character Pogo was right when he said, "We have met the enemy and they is us!" Do you hold self-limiting beliefs such as always assuming the worst in ambiguous situations? We are all products of our experiences, and we all have unique lenses through which we see our current situations. Mark Twain said, "A cat doesn't sit on a hot stove twice—but doesn't sit on a cold stove either." Were you "burnt" in the past by raising a disagreement with a boss and vowed never to do that again? Everyone who works for an organization has experienced power differentials in many forms, and these differentials exist even within families, schools, and social activities. Have your experiences with these distorted your interpretations and reactions to others' actions?

Where are you in dealing with authority? Do you tend to prematurely defer or "take up arms" at the first sign of leader imperfection? Does your attitude interfere with your ability to take a partnership orientation in dealing with those farther up the hierarchy? Can you raise dissenting views with those of much higher power? Are you generally overconfident so behave in inordinately risky ways, or do you lack self-confidence so too readily give away power? Do you underestimate the power you have, thereby increasing the power gap? A striking number of people do not use all the power or influence at their disposal.

Understanding the dynamics of power can help you see that much of the annoying behavior of those farther up, including their reaction to your low-power behavior, is due to the situation they are in. Recognizing this will make you less likely to demonize them.

Many—if not most—people have complex feelings about power in others and in themselves—something that makes it difficult to tell who really has power, and how much. This is why it's crucial to understand oneself well enough to be able to accurately assess both the powerful and one's own position in relation to them. Lower-power people must be able to estimate how much power another person actually *has* in order to change their relationship. To understand another person's power, you have to know several things: who they are connected with and their relative influence with each, the resources they control or can access, and the information they possess or can readily obtain. You can figure out some of this via observation, some by reputation, and some by investigation.

Having that external knowledge provides the basis of influence. The more you understand what concerns senior managers, the better chance you have of determining how to get their attention and gain their cooperation. You have influence insofar as you can speak to the other's needs and concerns. That allows you to act like a true partner in setting up win-win exchanges.

The chapters to come will provide you with ways to increase your relative power so that you can have the influence that will allow you—and powerful people—to be their most effective. This doesn't include taking power from the powerful, because that would reduce their needed ability to lead—and organizations led by powerless people don't do very well. Rather, it's about learning to increase the total amount of power in the system, making both yourself and the powerful more able to do great work. The object is to help relatively powerful people use the talent that helped them become powerful, and help relatively less powerful make fuller contributions.

For now, we will mention that senior people in larger organizations may be less accessible than they are in medium to smaller organizations. So when influencing outsiders or people in larger organizations, you might need to spend a lot of time and energy on figuring out how to gain access. The larger the organization, the more removed senior people are likely to be from lower-power people—and therefore the more likely they are to manifest some of the worst aspects of power differential. But even in entrepreneurial start-ups without many employees or layers, founders may overvalue their own expertise, and undervalue that of others—which was the case with Chandran Menon, as we saw in Chapter 2. Regardless of the size of your organization, we will help you figure out how to gain the necessary access.

It would be irresponsible if we didn't fully acknowledge that it takes a certain amount of *courage* to put the lessons you will learn in this book into practice. The most skillful individuals and organization players can't get it right all the time, and aren't likely to get anywhere if they don't take risks. Careful analysis and skillful execution can reduce risk to some degree. But you need to be brave to try to influence people who are, by definition, more powerful than you are. Take heart; others have done it and you can too. That is the focus of this book.

The next two chapters introduce the steps required to influence powerful people, then Chapter 6 takes a closer look at the partnership mind-set. Subsequent chapters add to your understanding and knowledge of how to gain the influence you desire.

Nothing we can say will totally remove the risk, and there are certainly situations that are indeed hopeless. But in a world where adding value is the only protection for continued employment—and where the cooperation of powerful people is always critical—giving up before you start is perhaps the riskiest choice of all.

CHAPTER

4

Overview of the Steps Required to Access and Influence Powerful People

The shortest summary of how influence works is that *everyone expects to be paid back*. People allow others to influence them because they believe they'll get something valuable in return. Although it sounds a bit cold—as though the only reason people do anything is out of self-interest—the things that people care about vary greatly. Their desires range from the seemingly selfish—"becoming more able to give orders"—to the purely generous—"enjoying the feeling that comes from seeing others prosper."

How does this play out in organizational terms? Influencing a powerful person can be crude ("Support me on this or I will reveal your manipulation of booked sales") or subtle ("Wouldn't it be useful to be known as an early supporter of innovation?"); noble ("This project will help save lives") or raw ("Can you really afford to be seen as blocking our best talent?"). Whatever form it takes, influence always involves *reciprocity and exchange* in which the powerful person or group is willing to be influenced because they benefit in some way. Friends and close colleagues assume that sooner or later, one good turn deserves another. With those who we don't know as well, we might have to make the exchange much more explicit and immediate. But some form of reciprocity and benefit in return for giving what is requested always undergirds influence.

Everyone acts upon this tendency; reciprocity is the social glue that holds relationships together. But when you don't seem to be able to influence effectively, a model can serve as a reminder or checklist. Although the *concept* of exchange is fairly straightforward, the actual *process* is more complicated. When you already have a good relationship with another person, you don't have to overanalyze the situation or your approach. You just ask, and the colleague will respond if he or she can.

However, often it can be more difficult in other situations to influence a person or group, and you need to use a more deliberate and conscious approach. That is why this influence model—a careful diagnosis of the other's interests, assessment of the resources you possess, and attention to the relationship—can be so valuable. It's especially helpful when you're faced with an anxiety-provoking situation like making a risky new investment, introducing a product, or outsourcing a contract. These scenarios tend to limit your focus and the alternatives. The model therefore prompts you to stop and consider what steps you must take to gain cooperation.

We begin with an evolution of the *Influence without Authority* model that we presented in previous books that we now apply specifically to the powerful. We flesh this out with an example of how to use the model when dealing with a powerful boss. We discuss each step in detail (see Figure 4.1). The eight steps of the model are as follows:

1. Determine Who Has to Be Influenced

This step is fairly easy when you're trying to influence your boss. Just keep in mind that your boss must answer to a boss (or two, or three) of his or her own—who also needs to be influenced. It's also not always so clear nowadays exactly *who* everyone's boss is (as in matrix organizations or those geographically dispersed). This can become increasingly complicated when you're tackling a complex issue with senior people both in and outside of the organization. Who is the decision maker? Who influences that person? If you don't pick the right person or people, you risk wasting your efforts.

2. Assume That Each Is a Potential Partner

One of the greatest challenges you'll encounter is trying to influence someone who doesn't seem interested in cooperating. But rather than dismissing that person, assume that everyone you want to influence *could* be a potential partner—*if* you work at it. Begin by assessing whether you could form a working alliance with someone by determining whether you have any overlapping interests. You can use this same approach with your manager as well; if you assume that managers are partners with their direct reports, then the responsibility to make the relationship mutually beneficial belongs to both of you.

We observed a common problem among many who have tried to influence powerful people and at first were not successful. After one or two failed attempts, the would-be influencer begins to attribute something negative to the target person or group. Whether it is a growing conviction that the other party has a deficient character (perhaps they see the other person as "just not smart/caring/farsighted enough to see the benefit") or a suspicion of motives, they'll deem the unresponsive party as deeply flawed. The problem is that even though the would-be influencer doesn't voice this attribution, it shows through in subtle ways—and creates even more resistance. It is very hard to influence people who may sense that you think they are flawed or worse.

This is why it's best to see the other person as a potential *partner*. This can prevent you from too readily disregarding the other person and reminds you to look for mutual interests around which to collaborate. You give partners the benefit of the doubt when things aren't going well, and redouble your efforts to help the other person achieve his or her goals—even when their interests are not obvious. Although it's clearly easier to do this with some people than with others, you can never be sure how resistant the powerful person will be until you approach him or her directly.

Example of Converting a Difficult Boss into a Partner: Dealing with Dr. Death

Consultant Matt Larson tells the story of dealing with a seemingly impossible person when he was recruited by a client of the large financial services firm where he worked:

I had been recruited by CONSULTMORT, and was in the unique position of having the vice president of operations as my number one team member. This was unusual, since she ranked higher than me . . . But limited resources and a high-profile client required that the VP become involved.

Everyone in the organization feared this woman; her "charming personality" had even earned her the nickname "Doctor Death." As one of the most powerful people in the organization, she controlled all the resources for our service model. She also made people look foolish regularly—and I did not want to start off my career at CONSULTMORT by getting added to that list.

The man I replaced as the project head in my new role had a particularly awful relationship with Doctor Death—which didn't help me start off well. I received advice from other leaders—none of whom had been able to establish a positive relationship with her. So I decided to take a more (junior) partner-like approach.

My first step was to defer to her. I let her know that I recognized she was the expert around CONSULTMORT from the moment I started, and asked her opinion on my interaction with the client, which seemed to disarm her. "Dr. Death" needs to be recognized as the smartest person in the room, and I had no problem doing that—especially as the new kid. I wanted to do whatever it took to do the job correctly.

Once appeased, she started granting me latitude on the way I managed things. That allowed me to connect with and influence other team members. And although I would rather have eaten paint chips, I also began to develop a personal relationship with her. I spoke about myself in a self-deprecating way, which made her laugh—and share bits and pieces of herself. I wasn't a fan of her humor, but I laughed when I knew it would please her. I wasn't being inauthentic; I just needed this person to like and respect me to make my life easier and the project successful.

We both worked incredibly hard from the beginning, into the early hours of the morning—which she respected. I asked her if there was any work I could take off her plate or do to make the project go easier for her. She always said no, but my offers led her to see me as an asset—not as the adversary she sees in most people.

Doctor Death soon started telling people that I could handle things without her—something she hadn't done with the former project manager. This gave me more room to empower employees who previously feared her wrath. We delivered the project on time, and with an amazing amount of support from this woman. While I credit her for its success, I also credit myself for stroking her ego enough to allow me to get the actual work done.

Although getting past his boss's offensive personality wasn't easy for Matt, he did manage to develop a modest kind of partnership with her. Because he kept an open mind and showed genuine interest in her, he discovered qualities he hadn't expected. He showed how crucial it is to avoid stereotyping someone with a gruff exterior. Even the most powerful person has needs, interests, and vulnerabilities, no matter how hard he or she tries to hide them. If aspiring partners can show some vulnerability, it makes it easier for the potential partner to relax.

A helpful perspective to take is: "We are going to be partners who can mutually influence each other, even though you don't yet know it. But I am going to show you how this arrangement will benefit you and the organization."

The challenge is to keep this perspective even when you aren't sure about the basis for the partnership. Such a positive and supportive assumption, although unspoken, can prompt dialogue that might otherwise have quickly short-circuited possibilities.

3. Determine Their Power and the Power Gap

The degree of the other person's power will determine how you respond. Relatively high power requires more deference, formality, and slower relationship development. A lower differential of power might allow for more informality, directness, and egalitarian style. As always, be careful that you don't attribute more power than the other person has—as we warned against in Chapter 3—and do not underestimate *your own* potential power. Think about what you have to offer (or withhold) that can help you gain influence.

Because power can be a result of either a person's organizational position or their personality, determine in this particular instance whether it's either or both. If positional/structural, what resources does this person actually control? In turn, what access do you have to relationships, information, resources (which are ultimately the source of all organizational power)? How can this help you determine what you can do to diminish the power gap?

If the person's power is personality-based, is it because of the particular qualities this person has—or is it just because others have assumed the person is powerful, and have never tested this? Some individuals whom others fear actually turned out to be quite isolated from their organization. Once you determine this, you eliminate the power attributed to them.

The following are other questions you can ask to help determine a person's level of power:

- **Have they acquired power by seeing themselves as benevolent and willing to give favors for loyalty?** In this case, you should place yourself at the benefactor's mercy—but framed in terms of helping accomplish their objectives.

- **Do they exercise raw power too freely, or conserve it until absolutely necessary?** You may need to confront bullies, simply by refusing to back down. It is not a good idea to try to bully a practiced bully; just take the attitude that you will not be intimidated and prefer collaboration.

- **Do they exercise power behind the scenes or very visibly?** Those with regal offices and a wall of assistants may require a lot of overt deference, whereas less pretentious individuals are more likely to prefer directness and warmth, with only tacit recognition of their relative power.

You must look at all of these power factors with an eye toward your own sources of power. Have you been correctly assessing your own power? From this analysis, determine how large the gap is—and what does it tell you about the higher-power party's likely resistance and responses?

The next step in the influence model takes you deeper into the power analysis.

4. Diagnose the World of the Powerful, Their Currencies (What They Value), and Which Ones You Can Offer

To be able to make compelling offers for exchange, you want to know what the other person values. We call these *currencies*, because they represent what can be exchanged. This isn't always easy to determine. If it's someone with whom you have worked for a long time and know well, you can probably figure out what they value most. Some individuals' currencies are reasonably obvious. However, the further the person is from you, the more challenging is the task of discerning his or her currencies.

Though personality plays a role, what people tend to value at work often has to do with their situation. If you can determine how "their world" works, you'll be able to discern their currencies. You may want to test your assumption before acting on it; you'll know by the response if you're in the right territory. Of course, you can always *ask* the other person if you have a friendly relationship with them: "I need to understand better what matters to you so that I can be sure you get benefits from our collaborating on this task."

This can be difficult sometimes. Although most people continuously broadcast what is important to them, you must listen very carefully to their language and tone. These things usually hint at what this person values, which will help you determine any overlapping interests. There are also external sources you can check, such as public records, speeches, public policy statements, or industry information. The more you can learn about this person's possible interests, the better your chances of finding something valuable to exchange.

You can also examine the organizational forces operating on the person. People respond to a number of conditions present in their particular professional situation; so think about how each of these conditions determines likely currencies.

Some sources for deducing probable currencies are:

- **Their actual job.** What tasks do they perform? Do they spend a lot of time in the public eye, talking to stockholders, major customers, financial analysts, the press? Or do they focus internally, and spend time inspiring the troops, redesigning and implementing strategy, fixing the organization, meeting with peers, interviewing new hires, and the like?

- **Career pattern.** Are they using skills they've honed, or do they have to complete unfamiliar tasks? Have they worked in the same company/organization and industry for a long time or have they recently moved? Have they spent a good portion of their career working in the country where they currently live? Did they make a first move outside of a functional specialty or have they done many general manager jobs in the past?

- **Their reporting structure and boss(es).** To whom do they report? What leadership style are they subject to? What does their supervisor require them to do and know—both in detail and more generally? Are they expected to be more externally or internally focused? Do they report to or have direct exposure to a board of directors?

- **Measures and rewards.** How is their performance measured? How are they compensated? Salary? Bonus? Stock options?

- **Physical arrangements.** Does the person work in a closely guarded area? Are there several layers of people through which one must pass to gain access? Or do they operate in an open area and frequently mingle with employees? Is their space designed for conveying status, work centrality, global connections, or something else?

- **External views.** What critiques or evaluations have outsiders made about the organization in the past few years? What were the main points of criticism? Understanding these contextual factors can often help you make educated guesses about what a senior person cares about, regardless of personality.

If you get stuck, consult with someone who has perspective on the boss or context; you may need a bit of distance to find the openings. Of course, keep in mind that this advice may be counterproductive or not helpful, as it was in the case of Matt and Dr. Death. Know your sources, and listen for anything that indicates that these people may have had a hand in perpetuating conflict.

Most people vastly underestimate the number and range of currencies they can actually command for use. Table 4.1 displays a list of common currencies in organizational life that specifically take

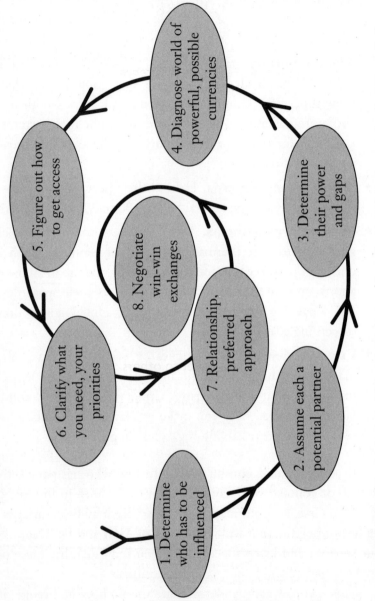

FIGURE 4.1 The Cohen-Bradford Influence Model (Expanded to Focus on the Powerful)

1. Determine who has to be influenced

2. Assume each a potential partner

3. Determine their power and gaps

4. Diagnose world of powerful, possible currencies

5. Figure out how to get access

6. Clarify what you need, your priorities

7. Relationship, preferred approach

8. Negotiate win-win exchanges

TABLE 4.1 Currencies Frequently Valued in Organizations, with Emphasis on the Powerful

INSPIRATION-RELATED CURRENCIES

Vision	Being involved in a task that has larger significance for unit, organization, customers, or society; chance to make a large difference
Excellence	Having a chance to do important things really well
Moral or ethical correctness	Doing what is "right" by a higher standard than efficiency

TASK-RELATED CURRENCIES

New resources	Obtaining money, budget increases, personnel, space, and so forth
Challenge/ learning	Getting to do tasks that increase skills and abilities
Assistance	Receiving help with existing projects or unwanted tasks
Organizational support	Receiving subtle or direct assistance with implementation
Rapid response	Getting something more quickly
Autonomy	Ability to work without close supervision; not have to answer to others
Information	Obtaining access to organizational or technical knowledge; being "in the know"

POSITION-RELATED CURRENCIES

Recognition	Acknowledgment of effort, accomplishment, status, or abilities; reaffirmation of importance
Visibility	The chance to be known by important people, higher-ups, or significant members of the organization
Reputation	Being seen as competent and committed; having integrity or national prominence
Insiderness	A sense of centrality, of belonging, a member of the elite
Contacts	Opportunities for connecting to other powerful people

(continued)

TABLE 4.1 *(continued)*

RELATIONSHIP-RELATED CURRENCIES

Acceptance/ inclusion	Feeling closeness and friendship; not being constrained by obligation
Understanding	Having others listen to your concerns
Personal support	Receiving personal and emotional backing, understanding the loneliness of a driver
Trust	Being ready for disclosure, assumed competence, delivering on commitments

PERSONAL-RELATED CURRENCIES

Self-concept	Affirmation of values, self-esteem, and identity; confirmation of their power or bragging rights
Gratitude	Appreciation or expression of indebtedness
Ownership/ involvement	Ownership of and influence over important tasks
Comfort	Avoidance of hassles

Note: This table appeared in both editions of *Influence without Authority* by Cohen and Bradford. It was originally derived from organizational observations over many years, with the five categories consolidated from much longer lists.

powerful people into account—almost all of which are available to anyone. Only some "hard currency" task resources might be difficult to generate; if you don't have a budget or personnel working for you, and that's what the person wants in exchange for help in supporting a project, then you can't immediately trade. No one wants all of these; nevertheless, even powerful people have broad portfolios of currencies they value. If you haven't got one thing, you might be able to find another.

5. Figure Out How to Gain Access

Even though your boss is generally easier to access than other higher-powered individuals, an overloaded or geographically distant supervisor can make this difficult. One example of this difficulty occurred with some managers at Montefiore Hospital; they admitted that the only way they could get any time with the incredibly busy, world-famous doctor who was their director was by studying his schedule, then hanging out near his office looking like they were reading the bulletin board, so they could bump into him and quickly do business as he was leaving or arriving. Bosses who live in different places from their direct reports can be hard to access for extended conversations.

There are a variety of ways to get around this problem. Finding the answers to a few questions will help: To access this person, do you have to get through a gatekeeper, with whom you will need to develop a relationship? What media do they use to get information? Would they prefer a handwritten note? E-mail? Social media? Are there conferences they attend, or clubs, boards, or charitable activities in which they participate? Are there friends who have access that you can influence to help? It can require a campaign, which is just as systematic as any other business activity—but don't be afraid to undertake this.

6. Clarify What You Need and Your Priorities

It's not always easy to determine what you want from a potential partner. Asking the following questions can help you figure this out:

- What are your primary versus your secondary goals?
- Are they short-term or long-term objectives?
- Are they "must-haves" or "nice-to-haves" that can be negotiated away?
- Is accomplishing this task or improving the relationship your priority?

Know your core objectives; this will prevent you from getting sidetracked into pursuing secondary goals. What are your priorities among several possibilities—and what are you willing to trade off to get the minimum you need? Do you want cooperation on a specific item, or would you settle for a better relationship in the future? People who desire influence frequently fail to distinguish their personal desires from what is truly necessary on the job—which creates confusion or resistance. For example, if you merely want to be seen as the smartest person in the room all the time, your personal concerns might interfere with more important organizational goals. (Former president of Harvard Larry Summers reportedly suffered from this problem and created massive faculty opposition because he had to win on even minor matters—not a great strategy when dealing with Harvard professors.) Would you rather be "right" or effective?

7. Diagnose Your Relationship and the Preferences for How to Approach

A good prior relationship makes it easier to ask for what you want without having to prove good intentions. If, however, the relationship has a history of mistrust—or no history whatsoever—proceed with caution. You will need to build the requisite credibility and trust required to engage.

Every person has ways in which they prefer others relate to them. Some like to see a thorough analysis before beginning a discussion; others would rather hear preliminary ideas and get a chance to brainstorm. This isn't about the style *you* prefer. If you operate according to the other person's inclination, you will have more influence.

For example, ask yourself the following about your boss's style: does he or she prefer openness, brevity, warmth, formal distance, overt respect? Does he or she focus on task and relationship first, or data and conclusions first? Over the years we have developed what we call the 15 percent rule: be 15 percent (that is, just a little) more open or vulnerable than you think the other person is ready for. This may require coming across as being tougher, more direct, terse, relaxed, more (or less) certain, or something else that isn't necessarily automatic behavior for you.

Everyone responds better when they are approached in ways that they prefer. In this sense, as in many others in the influence process, *it is better to follow the Platinum Rule rather than the Golden Rule: instead of "do unto others as you would have them do unto you," it is often more effective to "do unto others as they want to be done unto."* As George Bernard Shaw pointed out, after all, they may have very different tastes!

For example, consider the experience of the head of production, Juan, at a furniture manufacturing company. According to Juan's chief executive officer (CEO), "He drives me crazy. I am walking down the hall and he grabs me and asks for $55,000 for a new cutting machine. If he would only write me a memo giving the details, of course, I would agree; but now I want to resist." Juan is operating in production world mode—in which he must make decisions immediately. He trusts his instincts rather than financial analysis, which Ken clearly would prefer. If Juan reflected, he would realize that the CEO, who came up through finance, would want facts and figures cleanly laid out. Juan lost influence because he related in a way in which *he*—not the other person—was comfortable.

8. Negotiate Win-Win Exchanges

Once you have determined what goods or services can be exchanged, you are ready to offer what you *have* in return for what you *want*. Your approach depends on the following:

- The attractiveness of your resources
- The partner's needs for what you have
- Your desire for what the partner has
- Your organization's or the powerful person's organization's unwritten rules about how explicitly people can express what they want
- Your prior relationship with the potential partner, as well as his or her preferred style of interaction
- Your willingness to take chances to pursue what you want

Planning for an actual exchange can be a challenge. When dealing with your boss, you have the advantage that a part of the formal role is to think about how to help you be most productive. Sometimes it is possible to just have a direct offer: "If I do X, then will you do Y?" But many bosses (and especially those farther up), take offense to being "bargained with." They assume that you doing X is part of your job, and therefore the behavior should not be offered as something to exchange. An explicit request can feel like "arm's-length negotiation" not appropriate to the boss-subordinate role—and the resentment that ensues can create distance between you and your boss.

But let's suppose your work requires some additional support. You can ask for it in a way that includes the boss's goals: "I would be glad to take on that project. However, that is going to require some additional expertise in order to make it work well. Can I utilize Denise who is knowledgeable in that technology to assist me?" You are not making the demand just because you want to get "paid" for your effort, but because it will help improve the final result.

As we have stressed, speaking to your boss's needs is more likely to lead to a successful outcome. For example, "I realize the pressure you are under from your boss on the numbers, so I will more closely manage to budgeted targets. However, in order to do that, I need to eliminate some of the busywork we now do that really isn't crucial. Can we stop doing X and Y in order to free me up to hit these critical targets?"

In many cases, you can "give two for the price of one." Is it possible that what you want is *also in your boss's* best interests? For example, let's say you want more discretion. Rather than saying, "I would be glad to take on that project if I can have autonomy on how to achieve it" (a "bargain" your boss is likely to reject), you could say: "Taking on that new project is fine. Presently, I have to check a lot of details with you, which wastes your time and is a bit frustrating for me. Can we agree on the critical issues that require check in? This will keep me from loading you down with all the details and free me up to do this important project."

Often the agreement is more implicit. Suppose it's crunch time, and you are working overtime. You don't say so, but you expect some compensation in the future. There is a problem, however, with such implicit agreements. If you fail to articulate this expectation, it's possible that your boss has a different understanding of what you want. Is there a way that you can convey the currency in which you want to get paid? For example: "I know that there is a lot of grunt work that needs to get taken care of during this crisis and I am more than glad to do it. I hope that when the pressure is off, you will look for ways to give me more challenging assignments."

These efforts are part of ensuring that the exchange is equitable. Are you getting justly compensated for your efforts? Sometimes it is smart to invest—go the extra yard to build up goodwill. But whatever the currencies (and whenever the payment), each side needs to feel that over time it is fair. The problem is that the requester is likely to underestimate the cost to the other, and the recipient of the request is likely to overestimate the benefit to the requester.

How do you protect yourself from being short-changed and convey the cost without sounding like you are whining? Be careful that you don't send the wrong signals. Here's an example: On Friday afternoon, your boss drops a big assignment on your desk that is due Monday morning. You cheerfully take it up, because you have no choice—even though you had personal plans that weekend that you now have to cancel. On Monday morning, you hand in the completed work to your boss. She thanks you, but do you say, "Oh, it was nothing"? That would convey that you don't expect much compensation (but wouldn't you be upset if you weren't fairly "paid"?). As we said, you don't want to whine, but there's nothing wrong with being honest. It might be enough to say, with a smile, "Yes, it took the weekend, and some flak at home; but I knew how important it was and wanted to help."

Sometimes you don't discuss the exchange; you just see what you need to do to get the kind of response you prefer, and start doing it, trusting that reciprocity will kick in as your efforts are noticed and appreciated.

Think about dual goals that align with the strategy you use—goals that will get you what you want, and help you achieve a partnership with your boss or higher-up. Don't win the battle but lose the long-term war because you have made your relationship more distant and hierarchical. It is always better to frame an agreement in positive terms that put the burden on you: "Good, so you can include me more when I (deliver X, or demonstrate greater unit concern, or learn to do Y, etc.)". That is part of deferring to the senior partner's role, but it also places responsibility on you, which makes the other person less defensive.

And always give the partner an out: "I know you can't guarantee a promotion/particular position or assignment/much greater availability, but I will keep my word, and trust that it will work out over time."

This model also can explain how people lose influence, and therefore fail to become a partner:

Ways to Lose Influence

- Forget an important stakeholder.
- See the other person as recalcitrant or un-influenceable at the first sign of resistance.
- Misread the power gap—either by assuming it is so large that you can't try, or so small that you're insulting the other person.
- Don't understand the other's world (e.g., assume they value *your* currencies).
- Think only of technical correctness, ignoring others and their concerns.
- Be unclear about your priorities.
- Fail to recognize currencies at your disposal.
- Relate to the other using an approach with which *you* are most comfortable.
- Misuse exchange (e.g., take, but don't give; give, but are unclear about what you expect in return).
- Overlook opportunities to build trust before you want anything specific.

With all this said—you don't have to get it perfectly the first time. This model also lets you recover when you initially hit a dead end. To help make these concepts more concrete, we describe in the next chapter a situation involving a controlling boss that seems impossible to overcome. You'll see how Doug, the direct report, was able to turn things around using this model.

5

The Influence Model at Work
Moving a Tough Boss

Is there any way to resurrect a relationship that seems to have "gone south"? The following actual situation illustrates how using the Cohen-Bradford Influence Model can turn around what appears to be an irreconcilable impasse. (One of the authors was able to debrief each of the parties; the dialogue is reconstructed from their combined memory of the conversation.)

This example involves Warren, the president of U.S. Operations at a large, multinational corporation, and Doug, the national sales manager for the United States who reports directly to Warren—and who isn't happy about how Warren manages him. The two men had a conversation about the sales operation and it did not go well. Doug then decided to go to Warren's office again to discuss their troubled relationship—and the discussion turned out worse than their earlier conversation.

Doug: Warren, have you got some time? I want to talk about that meeting we had the other day. We need to deal with the way we work together. I think it's interfering with our ability to get things done.

Warren: You're probably right about that. Go on.

Doug: I've been in sales for over 15 years now, but you treat me like a new hire, and question my judgment every time I do something. I'm a national sales manager, and I want to make decisions in my own area. You seem to be constantly looking over my shoulder and micromanaging me.

Warren: Well Doug, now that you've mentioned it, I *can't* always trust your judgment. If I just listen to what you tell me, I'd have to believe that your sales force can do no wrong. I never really get the whole story from you—just the good news. I only seem to hear the problems in sales when I dig for them myself.

Doug: Do you want news bulletins from the front line every 5 minutes?

Warren: No Doug; that's not the issue. Trouble is you go off and make important decisions on your own that I only hear about when it's too late. You never even ask my advice about anything.

Doug: You don't give me the chance, Warren. Take last month when I was trying to deal with Marty's poor results. You got word of it somehow and you jumped in before I'd figured out how I was going to handle it.

Warren: But Doug, you've never given me any bad news about Marty. Like I said, when you only tell me the good stuff about people, you imply that they can do no wrong. I have no sense how big the issue is when I hear about these situations; I need to find out what's going on.

Doug: Well, if I do give you the bad news, it haunts the person forever. I've got to protect my people. It's incredibly difficult to change your mind once you've locked in an opinion.

Warren: You've got to be able to look beyond your own department's interest. You only see things from the sales point of view.

Doug: It's my job to represent sales! If I don't do that, who's going to? Besides, you never listen to me or support me, so I have to push.

Warren: Yes, representing sales is part of your job—but only part. I need you to be a team player with an open mind, not just an advocate for your own limited perspective.

Doug: Okay. Okay. I could be a better team player. But my team feels like they're all stuck in left field.

Warren: Well they'd feel less out there if you involved me more frequently. I can troubleshoot and share the big picture with them if you were less protective of your turf.

Doug: I think you've missed my point.

Warren: I guess we're just very different people with very different management styles.

Clearly, these two are not in a good place. Doug has given up on trying to change the conditions with Warren. But all is not lost. The issues are out on the table; however, both men are convinced that the other refuses to change. If they don't address the situation, the best they'll have is an arm's-length relationship marked by low trust and little mutual assistance. Before exploring how they can fix this situation, we should explore what went wrong. The influence model gives us some clues.

1. **Doug is not seeing Warren as a potential partner.** Warren offered an opening to Doug ("I can troubleshoot and share the big picture"), but Doug didn't hear that. Instead, he sees Warren as a micromanager who can't be influenced. And although Warren did seem a bit difficult to influence, Doug didn't attempt to determine whether this was as absolute as he thought.

2. **Doug didn't try to understand Warren's world.** Part of the value of getting the issues out in the open is that we know what Warren wants (his "currencies"):

   • The whole story about what is going on; not just good news

   • To know how big an issue is

   • Doug to ask his advice where he can make contributions

   • To be invited to troubleshoot where needed; to share the larger picture with the sales force

   • Doug to be a team player; look beyond sales to the whole organization's needs, not just advocate for sales

   Doug didn't consider why Warren had those needs. Isn't it likely that Warren doesn't want to be surprised if he were questioned by his boss and would have to admit that he knew nothing about the situation? Isn't he accountable for the sales group's performance? And aren't these legitimate situational pressures? As we have noted, most people blame another's personality ("Warren has high needs for control"), failing to consider how important the *situation* is.

3. **Doug didn't see where his behavior was partially causing Warren's response.** Figure 5.1 shows that Doug and Warren are in a lose-lose exchange. Though neither can remember *when* this started or *who* started it, each person has legitimate concerns (currencies)—even though they trigger an undesirable response in the other.

   Seeing this as an interactive "system" does several helpful things. One is to get each party to stop making negative motivational (and personality-based) attributes about the other. Warren may not be an anal micromanager who hates sales and sees the world only in negative terms. And Doug is probably not counter-dependent, operating with limited perspective and paternalistically needing to protect his staff.

The second advantage of recognizing these reciprocal impacts is that it is an easier and safer way to raise the issue. If Doug accuses

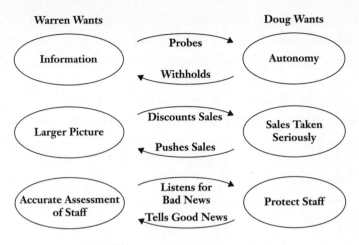

FIGURE 5.1   Negative Exchanges

Warren of being a power-hungry micromanager, he's in danger of making a serious career-limiting move. However, he could instead describe the dynamics of their relationship:

Doug: Warren, I have been thinking about some of the problems we have had in working together and I think we are in a lose-lose place. As the national sales manager, I need to run my shop—that is my job. But I think my need for autonomy has led me to hold back a lot of information, which must drive you crazy.

Warren: Damn right. It keeps me in the dark. I have to know what is going on; that's *my* job.

Doug: I appreciate that and am sorry. I can now see that my withholding information gets you to probe, and the more you probe, the more I want to withhold to preserve my autonomy. That's our screwed-up dance.

Doug could then go on and point out the other two cycles, which opens the door for some joint problem solving. This allows each to get what he wants without frustrating the other. Yes, it does require that

Doug admit his part of the problem; but most bosses want their junior partners to do this.

In the best of all possible worlds, Warren would take the initiative to try to improve the relationship. After all, Doug is a very important subordinate and Warren would benefit from an open, collaborative relationship. Unfortunately, Warren didn't initiate—and he wouldn't be the first boss to become angry at a subordinate and not tell him. Because our goal is to show how the person with less power can change things, we will pursue the possibilities from Doug's view—and use the "influence without authority" model to see what ideas emerge:

- **Determine who has to be influenced.** Doug has a choice. He could complain to Warren's boss about how he is managed. However, that is a high-risk strategy and one he should use only as a last resort. He can talk to others about how terrible Warren is, but that provides only temporary relief and has its own risks. He can quit, which is costly in many ways. The best option would be to exhaust all possibilities in building a positive relationship with his manager. Because Warren has an open door policy, Doug only has to ask for a meeting to get it.

- **Assume that each is a potential partner.** Doug might find this difficult, since he's convinced that Warren cannot be influenced. But he has to let go of the victim role. Furthermore, like many upper middle managers, Doug appears to desire total autonomy from his boss—not partnership. He can't fathom moving from independence to interdependence. One of the ways to make the transition to real collaboration is to consider how the other might be influenced.

- **Determine their power and the power gap.** Although Warren has a lot of power, Doug is not without a significant amount as well. He holds a vital position, has a strong track record in sales, and is also willing to raise the important issues. Warren's blunt and direct style reflects a considerable amount of personal power; however, he doesn't use it to coerce or ignore Doug, or compel him to give up. And Warren's acceptance of Doug's bluntness in return signals that Doug doesn't have to beat around the bush, which increases his ability to influence.

- **Diagnose the world of the powerful and their currencies.** Warren has overtly stated what he needs. Doug is high enough in the organization to know that a norm for senior executives in this company is "in order to look good, you need to have an answer for your boss's questions." He is also aware of the relationship that Warren has with his superior. He ought to realize that Warren has to keep current on how all parts of the North American operations connect. Doug needs to reflect on this a bit to understand Warren's concerns.

- **Gain access.** In this case, all Doug had to do was ask for another meeting; there is no sign that Warren wouldn't be open to one if it could be productive.

- **Clarify what you need (and priorities).** In the heated interchange between the two of them, Doug has also telegraphed what he wants.

  - Respect for his years in sales
  - Not having his judgment constantly questioned
  - Autonomy: the right to make decisions in his own area
  - Not be micromanaged by Warren
  - Warren not to hold on to impressions; be more open in changing his mind
  - Warren to support Doug in sales

But what is the relative importance of each? Are there others (such as building trust and a partnership relationship)? Which ones are the most important and what of these is Doug willing to forego?

- **Define the nature of the relationship (and how each wants to be related to).** Obviously, this relationship has little mutual trust. Doug will have to be specific in his exchanges in order to establish clear accountability and a way of keeping track of each one's end of the bargain. On the other hand, he is learning that he can be direct with Warren and not have to worry about being delicate or indirect in what he says. Warren isn't warm and fuzzy, but he doesn't act defensive and threatened.

- **Work out win-win exchanges.** The objective is not just to engage in a concrete exchange, such as "give more information in return for more latitude," but to build a partnership relationship as well. This moves it from an "arm's-length" negotiation ("I will give you X if I can get Y") to "how can we work more closely together?" Doug must also decide what issue to address first. Should he get more difficult matters out of the way immediately, or build up to these by discussing less critical matters? What is Doug willing to commit to? As the subordinate, he will probably have to agree to certain behaviors before he gets the responses he wants from Warren.

The previous analysis covered some of the issues that Doug pondered (while getting some coaching). The process led to this actual follow-up meeting with Warren:

Next Meeting

Doug: Warren, can we try this again? I've been thinking about our discussion the other day. It couldn't have been very satisfying for you, and it sure wasn't for me.

Warren: You're right about that.

Doug: I'd like to see if we can't figure out a way for both of us to get what we need; as pilot and copilot, we need to fly in the same direction. This is no way to run an airline.

Warren: So, what do you suggest?

Doug: Well first of all, let me make clear what's bugging me and try to understand what's bugging you. This might help us find some common ground.

Warren: That sounds okay to me. But I won't sign blank checks. I'm not willing to abdicate my responsibilities here.

Doug: I'm not asking you to do that. I just need to feel that my 15 years in sales have earned me some respect for what I know. I need to feel that you trust me to make more than the trivial decisions, and I need you to support me in these decisions.

Warren: [More firmly] I said no blank checks. I can't just hand over the reins to you.

Doug: I'm very clear on your need to feel that things are under control, and I realize that you get very uncomfortable when you don't have the information you need. Without a sense of what's going on, and assurance that I've done the hard analysis, you can't give me the sort of freedom I want.

Warren: Data, Doug; that's what anybody in my position needs. I have to base my reports on specific information.

Doug: I know you're held accountable for the numbers. But do the folks above you ask you the sort of detailed questions that you ask me?

Warren: Look, the only way they can manage a company this size is to stay on top of the numbers. They have to challenge everyone's assumptions and be confident that the analysis is sound, and so do I.

Doug: Okay. I'll be sure that you get what you need from me, and maybe we can keep them off your back together. But I'm going to need some things in return.

Warren: Like what?

Doug: Can we decide upon crucial areas where you need to review my decisions, and perhaps grant me some autonomy in others?

Warren: Sure Doug; that makes sense. But it's going to take more than that to work out all our issues.

Doug: I can see that. I'm happy to give you more information earlier, but I worry that you'll become overinvolved and make the decisions for me.

Warren: I don't *want* to make the decisions for you! I really want to honor your position as national sales manager. I just want to give some input when I have something to offer.

Doug: Okay; but what should we do when I feel you've moved beyond opinion giving to decision making?

Warren: Well, you could tell me that, you know. I don't mind having you push back at me, because then at least we have something to talk about.

Doug: Hmm, well that seems fair enough. Let's try it.

Warren: Sounds like we've got a deal.

Even though Doug is the subordinate, he took the initiative in this conversation. And although Warren wasn't initially very receptive and could have been seen as resistant, Doug persisted—and he kept speaking to Warren's needs and concerns. He also implied a desired partnership by referencing "pilot and copilot."

However, Doug could have developed this further. He didn't get all of his needs met, nor did he address all of Warren's concerns. Perhaps he assumed he should be happy with what he got, or worried that Warren might think him too demanding (although Warren didn't seem to). Doug settled for an okay resolution—thereby making the subsequent relationship only okay. It won't be the partnership it could have been.

What else might Doug have done?

First, he didn't have to let the conversation end there. When Warren said, "Sounds like we've got a deal," Doug might have said: "Yes and I think this is a good start. But I think that there is more that we can do so that we can better work together."

Warren: Such as?

Doug: You said the other day that you would like to give the big picture to my people. I think it would be very useful if you could attend our weekly meetings once a month, and address some major issues the company is facing.

Warren: I'd be glad to.

Doug: Good, I'll set that up with your administrative assistant. You're welcome to stay for the rest of the meeting; I just wouldn't want you to get too involved in our issues. It is in both of our best interest that you let us do the heavy lifting.

Warren: I can agree to that, as long as you don't object when I have some particular knowledge that would help in the decision—if you're amenable to my engagement on major issues.

Doug: Fair enough; no reason why we should lose your expertise. You also said that you want me to not *just* represent sales. I agree with this; part of my job as a senior executive is to take account of other areas. It will be easier for me to do that if I get some support from you in regard to our challenges in this tough market, so that I don't feel that I have to do that alone.

Warren: I'll do that, but it is crucial that you look beyond sales.

Doug: Yes. And I realize that words are cheap and that I will have to demonstrate that to convince you. There's just one more issue I want to address, and it has to do with personnel matters. I want to get your advice on some of the more pressing challenges, since you have a lot of experience. However, I don't want you to immediately begin thinking negatively of whoever we are talking about. I find it difficult to change your mind when you lock into a certain judgment. What can we do about that?

Warren: Well, I don't think I do that; I just need new data. But if you think I am, call me on it. I don't mind you pushing me. Then we can discuss it.

Doug: Okay, that's fair enough. I think we have gotten all the issues out on the table. If we can implement these, then I think we will be pilot and copilot flying in the same direction.

Doug was smart enough to point out that "words are cheap," and that the subsequent actions are what counts. Although this conversation is only a start, you can begin to change your relationship by letting your boss know that you realize what he values and want to give what he wants. You can build a little bit of trust through the openness of the dialogue. However, you can only develop deep trust if each party honors their commitments.

There are several important conclusions to draw from this.

1. **You don't need complete trust to have this sort of conversation.** Rather, trust will come about because of the actions you both take afterward. Doug approaches Warren by addressing the need to meet Warren's concerns and determine his desires from Doug; it's not particularly "soft." Warren doesn't hold back either, and they push on each other in an open, problem-solving way. Openly addressing valued currencies—and how to give for what you receive—tends to build a degree of trust. It's an outcome both parties can strengthen as each delivers what was promised. And the more each delivers, the better the partnership.

2. **The influence model allows for an open discussion of the issues with a minimum of accusation.** The desire to understand the other's currencies in order to work out win-win exchanges is quite different from seeking to prove that your label for the other is right.

3. **You don't have to stop early—or before your needs are met—when giving others what they want.** Doug was wrong in thinking that he had to stop prematurely for fear that he might be seen as asking too much. He was giving Warren what Warren said he wanted; he therefore could have given more and requested more.

4. **Despite their effectiveness, conversations like this don't ward off all future problems.** Despite their good intentions, Doug will probably feel as though Warren interferes sometimes.

And Warren will occasionally believe that Doug sometimes is withholding crucial information. But if they use the influence model, each of them can discuss those incidents when they occur.

The danger for the Dougs of the world occurs the first time he thinks Warren is interfering. Rather than assuming that this person *is* just an intrusive micromanager, Doug should use this opportunity to explore the issue further. Maybe they weren't clear on the vital issues or central information. Doug might say something like: "Warren, I want to do a 'time-out' on this task discussion, because I feel like we're getting too much into the details. This seems like we're going beyond the major issues we agreed to discuss during our meeting, and getting into the minor. Am I missing something?"

Warren might catch himself and agree that he has overstepped the line; or, this could lead to greater clarity. In either case, Doug shows that he is committed to making their work relationship as mutually beneficial as possible—and not trying to eject Warren from the cockpit.

5. **Don't just fix the immediate problem; discuss in a way that builds toward partnership.** Doug didn't quite see the opportunity as one where he could both solve problems and build a partnerlike relationship with his boss. This has the potential of Doug increasing his power while allowing his boss to get closer to the action—a paradoxical outcome that hadn't occurred to him. He simply saw a struggle to preserve his power by increasing his autonomy, even at the expense of Warren's confidence in him. A bigger opportunity to create interdependence was looming ahead of him—he simply didn't see it.

Doug did make progress without acting phony or "kissing up" to Warren. He was straightforward, and did not resort to what many people do when dealing with powerful people: using the "sandwich" technique by surrounding a negative statement between two nice ones or compliments. The recipient in this situation recognizes it as a setup. And because it can come across as insincere, it lowers trust. Furthermore, it is ineffective because the recipient tends to ignore the compliments and overfocus on the negative. The only thing this approach accomplishes is to put more distance in an already nongenuine relationship.

There are of course other difficulties when direct reports try to work out difficulties with their manager, issues we explore in Chapters 7 through 10. But before doing that, we need to flesh out more fully what exactly we mean by "being a partner"—which we do in Chapter 6.

Building a Powerful Partnership with Your Boss

6

Partnership

The Critical Mind-Set to Overcome Power Gaps

Is it really possible to form a partnership with a powerful or antagonistic person? Yes, it is! And we'll tell you how. First, it will help if we explain just what we mean by partnership, why it is important, and how it can improve your influence attempts.

The Gaps That Make Influence Necessary

Organizations have power differentials built into their structure. Roles come with varying levels of formal authority and varying access to resources, support, and information; these differentials are necessary for organizations to function. Nevertheless, large power differentials can frustrate those in the lower positions.

This is the case in most subordinate-boss relationships. The parties are supposed to work together, but that often becomes problematic. Though specifics vary from one organization to the next, there are a variety of ways to overcome these issues. The best way by far is to aim for a true partnership with the higher-power person. Whether or not this partnership actually happens, it is important to at least try. If successful, you can build for the future and set the tone for influencing others.

The Meaning of Partnership

An experience of one of the authors presents a good example to use in defining "partnership." Years ago, a medium-sized law firm hired him to address some internal conflict. He began the intervention by conducting individual interviews, and he was struck by the way the lawyers said the word *partner* as if it was in quotation marks and italicized. The word was not simply the name of a title commonly used in law firms; it obviously had deep emotional significance to everyone. As frustrated as they were with each other, the lawyers had a special feeling about their partners—an almost sacred set of expectations—that became a lever for solution.

"Partnership" does not necessarily imply equality, nor does it discount organizational hierarchy. It may mean that you have to see yourself as a *junior* partner, allowing the senior partner to overrule when he or she feels obligated to do so. He or she still has the ability to fire, promote, allocate tasks, award bonuses—or even ignore you if you aren't a direct report. But a junior-partner/senior partner relationship has some critical components, which we discuss in the following section.

The Characteristics and Expectations of True Partnership

- Both partners **are committed to the organization's overall goals** (or to the mutual benefit of each other's organizations) **and**

to the success of the other. This means that a junior partner must look beyond his or her subarea to include the senior partner's concerns as well. This is a belief that "We are in this boat together; I am concerned with your success as well as my own."

- Your motives must be to (1) **help the partner,** (2) **help the organization,** and as a by-product, (3) **help you take on and succeed at challenging jobs or projects.** Personal advancement can't be your primary or dominant goal.

- Junior partners **must be proactive;** you can't just wait to be told what to do or how to do it. You must care about your potential partner's success so much that you can be honest with him or her—in a collaborative way, of course. It changes the definition of loyalty from "telling the boss what s/he wants to hear" to telling the boss what s/he *needs* to hear to be effective. It allows you to be on the other's side, even though it can be a bit uncomfortable.

- In turn, **you encourage the partner to be honest with you,** and do not manipulate or communicate by hinting or speaking indirectly. It's always best to be specific, and assume that the partner wants to know what is necessary to be effective.

- This **requires transparency,** because your (possibly) new behaviors—including communicating more directly—might make the other person question your motives.

- **You do not move away from the potential partner, even when there are difficulties or tensions;** you always **move toward,** thus recognizing the interdependence between manager and employee. You need your boss, and she needs you. You always want to improve your relationship, moving toward collaboration and mutual benefit, even when addressing specific problems.

- In response to your helping the boss, **bosses give honest feedback.** They help the junior partner learn and develop—not just judge. And, as a junior partner, you are open to your own learning and not seeing it as a sign of inadequacy.

- You must accept that the partner is human and therefore flawed, so **give him or her the benefit of the doubt.** You cannot write-off a partner after his or her first mistake or mystifying behavior. When you automatically label the other person as defective, stop, step back, and diagnose further. Many people initially cast a powerful person as impossible—the person may turn out not to be.

- You must also be open to **discussing the nature of the relationship.** Address what each person wants it to be, and what is or isn't working.

- Both partners **accept that there are differences between senior and junior partners.** After the junior partners have had their say, the senior retains the right to make final decisions and expect full commitment. Juniors work hard to make the right decisions and not hold back on unpopular views; however, they have to accept the senior's right to override.

- Partners **adapt to the degree of closeness each wants,** but they are not totally unwilling to be more vulnerable with one another.

The one thing a junior partner must *never* do is add to the senior's work or concerns. Rather, they should do everything they can to lighten the manager's load, all the while assuring them that they're committed to helping the organization operate as effectively as possible.

Operating from these assumptions can truly make a partnership productive and freeing to both parties. However, this isn't a guarantee that all powerful people immediately will welcome this approach. Your challenge will be to win the reciprocal partnerlike behavior from them.

This example not only illustrates the difference between acting like a partner and acting like a contractor; it also reveals how hard it can be for employees who've been conditioned to keep arm's-length to think in terms of partnerships. When you're dealing with someone who resists forming a partnership, your mind-set ought to be: "We are going to be partners even though you don't yet know it. But I am going to show you how this will benefit you and your organization."

Example of the Difference between a Partner and an Arm's-Length Provider of Services

After independent consultant Liam Fahey agreed to do a major project with a large company, he received a 17-page contract (obviously written by the purchasing department with major input from legal) that used the term *vendor*. Liam crossed out *vendor* and replaced it with *partner*, and the legal department asked him what the difference is. He replied, "Vendors try to screw you whenever possible. Partners are interested in working together to solve problems." The legal people reverted to type and said, "Keep the term *vendor*." (Eventually, senior executive friends of Liam's at the company overruled legal and wrote the word *partner* into the contract.)

Why Partnership Is Needed

We are working according to the premise that the old subordinate-superior model is dead—or at least should be. This type of highly constrained and hierarchical supervision inhibits direct reports who need greater latitude to contribute what bosses need. Leaders need to hear all relevant information, even when it goes against their beliefs. They must be able to count on those below to constantly find new ways to do things. Similarly, direct reports must challenge their managers when they're beginning to err.

A *partnership relationship* is of benefit to the boss, even though he or she may not always realize or accept this. This mind-set requires a transition for some managers—and part of a junior partner's job is to aid in that transition. And although few employees want their boss to tell them what to do all the time, some are ambivalent about taking up the responsibilities that are the outgrowth of true partnership with the boss. They long for autonomy, where they can do what they want and not just what they're told. Being an actual junior *partner* requires moving to interdependence—a situation in which both people have influence, and thus the size of the "power pie" is increased. This can provide considerable autonomy while allowing the junior partner to have more impact on the overall tasks, goals, and outcomes of the wider unit.

Both boss and subordinate benefit from partnership, because they will make better decisions, generate more ideas, and implement more plans collectively than alone. This prompts those below to voice their wish for more challenging work, autonomy, support, and coaching—whatever will let them excel. It is much easier to share these desires with a boss who's a partner than with one who is merely playing a prescribed hierarchical role.

Of course, subordinates still have to meet expectations; you may even have to complete tasks assigned by your manager that aren't exactly "your job." Yet solely meeting these expectations may not be enough to establish partnership with your boss—even if you meet them well.

Although some senior managers resist partnerships, they all need them. No one can fully predict what an organization might require, and employees should use every available process to accomplish the organization's goals. When managers don't know the full scope of the problem or can't come up with solutions, they need collaborative partnership from below or outside.

What Does Partnership Require from You?

First of all, partnership requires a change in mind-set. Some people become rather comfortable in the role as deferential subordinate. They can avoid responsibility, "delegate" the difficult problems upward, and then blame their superior when things go wrong. However, true partners do not act so passively, but instead take initiative to solve problems and seize opportunities when they see things not working. To paraphrase a top naval officer's words to a new sailor on his ship: "Son, I don't ever want to hear you say that the ship sank because sailors on the other side screwed up."

Junior partners must also be open to learning, receiving feedback, and thinking broadly with the organization in mind. They know they're never finished products, but organisms in a continuous state of learning. And they must of course see their partners in the same way.

Finally, partners must be willing to take risks—prudent risks rather than reckless ones, but risks nonetheless. Responsible partners must be ready to share bad news, raise uncomfortable business problems for which they have no solutions to offer, and tell the boss when his or her actions are causing problems. In fact, pointing out the very issues that threaten a relationship is what partners must do to preserve the partnership relationship. This makes "playing it safe" one of the greatest barriers to partnership—failing to discuss things is what keeps a true partnership from developing.

We've already cited some managers' preference to recoil from interdependence—which only guarantees that partnership will *not* develop. An example of this involves three nonprofit boards we have served on, whose presidents actively avoided contact with the board chair and other members. Even when they had to interact, these individuals did everything they could to keep the chair at arm's length; they withheld information, refused to seek advice, discouraged expression of expertise, and just seemed to hope that they would "go away."

Partners have to realize all the sources of power at their disposal. People frequently (and erroneously) think of power in terms of *hire, fire, reward, punish* or *promote*. However, the senior partner needs many things from the junior partner—as we discussed in Chapter 4—and those currencies that the senior partner needs are the key source of the junior partner's power and influence.

Whose Responsibility Is It?

Finally, the lower-power person has to accept that the responsibility for changing the relationship to *partnership* is his—a fact that can be hard to swallow. After all, the senior person has more power; isn't it *his* responsibility to establish an effective work relationship? The answer is yes, but it isn't exclusively the supervisor's responsibility. This question presumes the attitude that subordinates have traditionally taken: "I will wait to see what my manager does, and I will respond if he or she comes through."

One of the many problems with this mind-set is that it actually *increases* the power gap. The lower-level person is giving the higher-up all the power to determine the nature of the relationship. When junior partners own their responsibility for defining the relationship, power gaps diminish. If they take the wait-and-see approach, their managers are likely to assume that the junior partners have little to add.

This approach misses another important point: the senior person may be too busy to spend time building a beautiful relationship with you. After all, you are not the only person below your boss; and managers are concerned about the relationship with *their* bosses as well. Any partnership your boss builds alone would be done according to his or her style, without necessarily taking your needs into account.

What Does an Elusive Boss Look Like?

It is all too common (albeit unfortunate) for a subordinate to want feedback and coaching from a boss who simply isn't interested in—or available to—give this support. This is especially widespread in the overloaded, thinly staffed organizations that have emerged in the last several years.

Many employees ask in a rather generic way for time to receive feedback and coaching from their managers. They may say something vague like, "I'd like to know how I'm doing" or "Can we talk about my career plans?" It's highly unlikely that an overloaded boss—one with other subordinates, projects, and issues—will clear time, prepare, and give detailed, constructive feedback and advice. Even if doing so is part of their job, they still may not have or take the time.

This is why it is critical for an eager subordinate to do some focused thinking and preparation first. What are their passions and their values about work? Can they assess their own competencies and areas for potential growth? Do they have plans to develop lacking or absent skills? Do they know the requirements for more senior positions or roles to which they might aspire? On what *particular* areas/performance/skills do they especially want feedback? What specific help do they want from the boss?

Subordinates who take the time to answer these questions are often pleasantly surprised at how their seemingly uninterested bosses respond. Evaluation of themselves, revealing what they've found and demonstrating their interest in learning, reduces the boss's discomfort about how they might respond to feedback. In addition, self-analysis gives the boss a chance to cite specific examples that support or counter what employees think of themselves—thereby prompting ideas for learning and growing.

Of course, some bosses fail to act like partners—for a variety of reasons. Some can think only about meeting their numbers. Others believe that they had to make their way without this kind of help, so why should they make it any easier for those who report to them? Some feel threatened in the presence of a smart, high-potential person who knows or can do things that the boss can't. Some aren't patient and don't listen very well; they leap right to giving advice based on their own experience and prejudices without connecting to the specific subordinate and his or her desires. And there is the occasional boss who is just sadistic and mean, and won't help anyone unless he or she can gain an immediate payoff. Of course, employees must be careful about assuming nasty motives. There are often many other reasons that drive observable behavior, most of which are not deliberate desire to inflict pain. If the boss seems to not want partnership, that can become a source of inquiry, even with a boss who tries to force you back into an inferior position. Any such response can be met with a response such as, "Yes, that's your right; can you tell me more about what that means for how I should be loyal and help you when I see a problem?" Accept the currencies and work to understand how to meet them, which starts immediately to put you on a better footing.

The Partnership Approach Can Work with Senior Powerful People

Powerful senior people might resist attempts to partner merely because they don't think it's important to partner with people who have less power. They worry that they're wasting time, making themselves vulnerable, or losing some of the power "mystique" they may think necessary for leadership. They don't want to be overwhelmed with requests or demands that will be hard to turn down, or have others think they play favorites.

Nevertheless, approaching these people with the partnership mind-set and letting them know you want to collaborate with them might be just enough to distinguish you from others. A simple conversation could arouse enough curiosity to merit a second look, or raise the possibility that engaging with you could turn out to be beneficial and not just a giant nuisance.

More and more organizational arrangements—such as alliances, mergers, acquisitions, and consortia—require that partnerships be formed, seldom between people of identical power. People must cultivate this trust over time. The following interview with John Maraganore—chief executive officer (CEO) of the start-up Alnylam—provides insight into his company's success with partnership relationships.

Alnylam is a pharmaceutical/biomedical company with great potential scientific value due to some recent advances they've made. A series of partnerships with 10 major pharmaceutical firms, aimed at developing treatments for genetically caused diseases, is at the heart of the company's business model. This focus prompted us to ask Maraganore to talk about how they manage the long-term partnerships—some with companies that are bitter rivals with each other. As John explains:

We are in an industry that takes $1 billion to $2 billion of investment and 10 to 20 years to get to cash flow positive. The cost of clinical trials has gone up recently. Vertex—with a drug that's about to get permission to market—has spent over $5 billion and taken 20-plus years. That's a very long feedback loop! We are in our ninth year, have raised about $1 billion, and have invested about $600 million so far. We have a lot more to invest, and are still years from profitability. We are positive about our potential results, but there is no certainty. We know the science is really good, Nobel Prize winning, with the best minds we can assemble, and we think we are in a good time, probability, and cost scenario. We're aware of how long and how much capital it will take, and which clinical trials are likely to succeed.

Raising capital is my number one job. Pharmaceutical companies are the senior partner; we're junior. It goes beyond a transactional agreement; it's about the nature of relationships, common goals, and alignment of interest. This is the only way to make them work.

Partnership Requirements

You have to earn belief and trust to form a partnership. Though reputation is vital, so is the quality of the science you bring, as well as honesty and transparency. It is impossible to bamboozle this group of people; they know what valuable partnerships require—a quality interface, science integrity, openness and honesty around data, and humility regarding the potential results. Excessive hubris never works. The soft side is amazingly key. A high-quality social interface is very important. They enjoy interacting with you. While science is the price of admission, what matters is the relationships, and the way you explain the value proposition.

(continued)

(*continued*)

Learning about Potential Partners

You learn early on what makes each potential partner unique, the first of which is knowledge of the industry and being aware of who the critical person is; it's different with Novartis than Biogen, for example. You get this information from being on boards, hearsay, and just general communication. There are various ways to find out about companies; sometimes you do formal homework, calling colleagues, asking them questions about potential partnerships—what worked, who the key people are, who has to buy into the science, what business terms they prefer. It's a very small community, so you can gather information quickly.

We quickly learned that Roche was very anxious about our other partnership with Novartis, since the companies don't like each other. It was critical for me to interface with the CEO at the time, Franz Humer, and reassure him; that kind of issue was only resolvable CEO to CEO. Our head of corporate communication received a request from her Roche counterpart for me to speak with Humer. We immediately talked about a possible partnership, the potential of conflict with our existing partnership with Novartis, and after, he said he wanted to get together again. So we met at his apartment in New York City for 90 minutes, and we committed to do a partnership—all of which was completed in five weeks. We said, "Look, we are in business with multiple partners; we have to be able to separate one set of info and objectives from another." Humer needed the reassurance that came with looking me in the eye, and knowing he had my word.

I've never met Novartis's CEO, Dan Vasella, and our partnership with them took much longer—with 20-plus meetings on the science side alone. Their head of science, Mark Fishman, then made a recommendation because he had a personal interest in our science. We let Novartis know when we had signed an agreement with Roche.

We approach each key person differently. For instance, Franz is Swiss; Mark is not. Franz is a lawyer, older, a legend in the industry, who deeply understands the importance of innovation in a smaller company from the perspective of the needs of a larger company. He is very wise in that way. I was excited about meeting him; I was very aware of his history at Roche, succeeded by their partnership with Genentech.

Mark is American, an amazing scientist, out of academia. He came out of Mass General, brought in by Dan Vasella, to build his scientific institute here in Boston. It is harder to build a close relationship with him; it actually took five years. He can be distant; we always connect around science and data, which are what he cares about. Franz is not a scientist; he's a businessman who cares deeply about innovation. My contact is less frequent with him because of distance, and his role. Franz is a decision maker, Mark is a scientist.

I think I am the same person both times, but know that I have to approach each man differently. Franz is a very impressive man, more formalistic. Mark is impressive and formal too, but different. I e-mail Mark frequently, which is less appropriate with Franz. Mark, closer to my age, and I talk more about personal matters; Franz and I do so less.

You learn that your partner has certain gods; with Franz it is shareholders and the board, for Mark it is Dan Vasella; it's about how they look as a result of doing the relationship. They care a lot about not being seen as having done a bad decision. They want everyone to be a hit. They worry at a personal level what they will look like if a partnership decision is not turning out well.

Managing the Relationships: Formal and Informal Mechanisms

Juggling 10 partnerships is fairly difficult, as you might imagine, and requires quality processes to do it. We have a distinct relationship with and a map of each partnership.

(*continued*)

(continued)

> We give each of our employees the responsibility to do whatever they need to do to nurture a specific relationship—dinners, breakfasts, lunches, whatever—since we are the junior party and they are the senior party. Over time, our counterparts begin to see us as peers; we develop relationships based on mutual scientific, business, and human interests.
>
> We also have an internal head of alliance who is part of our management team; she attends weekly meetings, reports what's going on, issues, gaps (and about our eight other partnerships too). They are complicated relationships. Roche has evolved dramatically, because they wanted to spin out the unit to deal with cost cutting. Any of them can change dramatically. Plus they are ad hoc all the time.

There is a lot to learn from this scenario. Widespread contacts help identify possible partners, and can be a source of information about specific potential partners. In short, networks matter—and it's vital to study key players carefully for their interests or currencies. John Maraganore's observations about Mark Fishman, first and foremost a scientist, in contrast with Franz Humer, a businessman, provide him with a lot of helpful information. Although you don't want to stereotype, you can make some educated guesses about the other person's likely interests. Then you have to pay close attention to see what is revealed in the face-to-face interactions that disconfirms, confirms, or extends hypotheses.

Accepting that you are the junior partner is paradoxical; because it acknowledges objective power differences (like the difference between Alnylam, a promising start-up with potential but no profits or products yet, and giant organizations such as Roche and Novartis), trust increases and some of the power differences diminish.

Even if you are only interested in influencing one powerful senior manager for a project, relating with a partnership mind-set can eventually lead to greater influence. You must earn the right to be treated as a partner; however, it is often more possible than it may at first appear.

It should be clear by now how the influence model can help you tackle the problems caused by power differentials. You've learned about the various ways to gain cooperation, and the potential for using a partnership mind-set to overcome the obstacles posed by working with people of various levels. The next section of the book will zoom in more closely to the boss–direct report relationship and show you how you can overcome power differences in that relationship.

CHAPTER

7

Building a Partnership Relationship with Your Boss

The notion of being a partner with your boss is pretty intriguing; after all, who wouldn't want to have a relationship where:

- You can be open with each other—tell "truth to authority" and know that you are getting the same in return.
- You have the same goals rather than being at odds.
- There is the leeway to disagree with each other and work out your issues together.
- You can take initiative and don't need permission to complete tasks. And when your initiative doesn't work out, the negative outcomes don't get your manager into the "blame game."
- You know that your boss is genuinely interested in your learning and growth as well as your immediate performance.

Although it's nice to feel close to someone and have their approval, the major benefit of this relationship is that it allows you to more fully use your abilities to meet organization goals. Of course, you have to *want* to carry a major part of the responsibility. You might blame your boss for failing to establish a partnership with you in the first place; however, if you want something different, you have to figure out how you can get it. You're fortunate if you have a boss who will initiate this kind of partnership with you—but because you can't count on that from every boss, you should learn how you can generate this yourself.

You will be more convinced that this can indeed occur if you know exactly how to go about it, especially with a boss who doesn't seem eager to embrace the concept. That is the focus of this chapter, which provides the framework for how to build a true partnership relationship. The following 10 steps outline the process:

1. Examine your own beliefs for barriers.
2. Adopt a partnerlike mind-set.
3. Accept that your boss isn't and can't be perfect.
4. Assess the gap in power between you and your boss.
5. Stop giving away your potential power.
6. Understand your boss's world or specific situation.
7. Raise your concern in a direct but nonblaming way.
8. Acknowledge your part in any difficulties.
9. Accept your boss's concerns as legitimate.
10. Don't undermine yourself by:
    - Prematurely backing off
    - Getting defensive
    - Trying to assign blame
    - Not exploring what really bothers your boss
    - Failing to be specific about both of your action steps
    - Failing to agree how to handle sliding backward

1. Examine your own beliefs for barriers

The first step—examine your own beliefs for barriers—requires that you ask the following questions about yourself: Do I hold any beliefs or take any actions that inhibit partnership? Have I really made an effort to understand my boss's world? And how can I raise those touchy issues that prevent partnership? (In the next chapter, we will explore more fully how to deal with resistance.)

2. Adopt a Partnerlike Mind-Set

For this step, you don't need permission to change your own mind-set; you just need to change some common ways of thinking, including moving away from:

- "I am responsible for only my area and my boss is responsible for the overall picture" *to* "I am also concerned for the overall success of the unit."
- "My manager is responsible for his or her own success" *to* "I also should be concerned for whether my manager *is* inadvertently doing self-harm, and doing what I can do to help him or her be successful."
- "My boss should take the responsibility for making this relationship work" *to* "It's my responsibility as well."
- "This boss is hopeless" *to* "Before I give up, I need to do everything possible to create a working partnership."

These are related to a larger issue: leaders traditionally have believed that *they* hold most, if not all, the responsibility for the unit's success.[1] This allows direct reports to then take the approach that, "Okay, since my boss wants to be totally in charge, I'll let him earn the big bucks and I will worry only about my sandbox." Subordinates who operate according to this opinion are likely to blame the boss when he or she doesn't come through perfectly.

Leaders will be more successful if they stop saying, "I am the only one carrying the larger responsibility" and start saying, "How can both my direct reports and I feel responsible for the unit's success *together*?" Of course, the direct report has to want this expanded responsibility. The good thing is that you don't need your boss's permission to be concerned with the overall success of the unit. Just as leaders should ask themselves, "Why am *I* doing that?" so should junior partners ask themselves, "Why aren't *I* doing that?"

3. Accept That Your Boss Isn't and Can't Be Perfect

This shift requires that you can both accept the boss's flaws and acknowledge his or her strengths. Rather than criticizing, a junior partner must ask, "What can I do to help my boss be more effective?" Accepting others for who they are is often the beginning, not the end, of improvement.

One of the vital elements to being a partner is taking the risk of giving feedback to your manager—which isn't necessarily easy. (We will discuss this notion further in Chapter 8.) The other change in mind-set relates to the attitude you hold about authority—whether you are fighting for a sense of autonomy, feel counterdependent and resist authority, or fear disagreeing and automatically defer to authority. It's critical to remember that "your boss is not your father"—and partnership is possible only if you become comfortable dealing with authority.

4. Assess the Gap in Power between You and Your Boss

Once you are clear about your attitudes toward leadership, responsibility, and authority, you must ask some questions about power—specifically, how much power do you and the boss each have—and what is the power gap? We made the distinction between *objective* bases of power and the power that one individual gives to another in Chapter 3. The former refers to the formal authority inherent in one's position, as well as access to resources like money, people, and sources of information—all things that are difficult to change.

5. Stop Giving Away Your Potential

However, there is also the kind of power that is more malleable, which includes power that we give to others, or give to ourselves—and take away from ourselves. There are various ways that junior partners disempower themselves, as discussed in Chapter 3; these include assuming that the manager holds all the responsibility or that you should always defer to the manager. Another way that junior partners diminish their own power is to fail to fully understand the boss's needs and therefore fail to offer what the boss wants. Junior partners also can underestimate their positional power and not realize the power they could have because of the many ways their bosses are dependent on them. As we explained in Chapter 4, *exchange* is the basis for influence. It's fairly simple: do you have things that the boss needs that you can exchange for what you need? To do that well, it is crucial to understand your boss's world.

6. Understand Your Boss's World or Specific Situation

Chapter 5 laid out various dimensions to consider when understanding the other's world. In addition to the objective forces that affect your boss—his job's demands, how she is evaluated—it is important to recognize that as the direct report, you are also part of your boss's world. Are there ways that you unintentionally *contribute* to the problem? Does your boss micromanage—and do you withhold information in order to gain some autonomy? Does this prompt your manager to intrude more? (This is the type of "negative exchange" loop that Doug got into with Warren in Chapter 5.)

If you can think of this as an *inter*personal problem (rather than just a major character flaw in the boss), you can raise the issue in a way we will describe later. What is the relative priority in terms of your needs? Which ones are showstoppers, and which are nice to have but not imperative? And what is the effect of your requests on your boss? The best-case scenario is for your objective to be a benefit to your boss; at the very least, it should incur minimal cost to him. Your goal must be to make your boss's life easier, not harder.

7. Raise Your Concern in a Direct But Nonblaming Way

We assume that you have done your homework to move forward— assessed your assumptions about your own and your boss's roles, the way you tend to relate to authority, and the forces that drive what your manager cares about. However, keep in mind that even your best assessment is only a working hypothesis. You don't *really* know the boss's world with certainty; you are simply guessing what the actual pressures, concerns, and goals are. You don't want to assume that you're certain about what *really* drives your boss. You simply must invite an open conversation during which your manager will share this information.

The following is an example of a relationship in which the direct report had almost total autonomy—but endured a puzzling override by the boss on one decision. When Len Schlesinger was a faculty member at Harvard Business School, he spent several years working in an administrative role involving external affairs, reporting directly to the dean, John McArthur. As Len tells it:

> John is a really skillful person. He exercises all power completely quietly, never does anything overtly "powerful." He allows all who work for him to have material autonomy. He only once intervened

during the four and a half years I worked for him. Since the alumni constantly complained about the magazine, and I thought it was terrible, I was thinking of revamping it. John called me and said, "Please don't." I was confused, and assumed he was somehow uncharacteristically out of touch. He had to explain, "It's not for alumni; it's a vehicle to write about faculty that don't get any attention elsewhere. It communicates to people that the school loves and respects them. I don't much care what alums think of it!"

Often, as in this instance, the powerful person also sees the problem, but defines it differently. This is an archetypal issue; from below, the powerful person's behavior seems resistant or irrational, but he or she is likely just using different criteria to judge the situation. The challenge is to figure out when that is the case, and when the powerful person is just being stubborn. Because McArthur so seldom gave orders, it wasn't hard for Len to inquire. But think of your situation: haven't you ever encountered an edict that at first seemed dumb but turned out to be not as arbitrary as you first thought? That's why it's vital to check your diagnosis.

One of the ways to escape the trap of false certainty is to develop multiple (reasonable) explanations for your boss's behavior. Assume that she is acting *reasonably* from her perspective, and then consider the situational reasons behind the actions. It is crucial to preserve the orientation by reminding yourself:

My manager is a potential ally; we have the same goals.

I am committed to my boss's success as well as my own.

The purpose is not to prove who was right or wrong in the past, but to work out how it can go well in the future.

These are tough mind-sets to maintain, especially if there has been a series of negative interactions. However, if you have the mind-set right, the right words will follow.

But it isn't always just the boss who needs to learn from examining his or her own behavior.

8. Acknowledge Your Part in Any Difficulties

There is another assumption you must make. No matter how egregious your boss's behavior seems to be, consider the possibility that you are in some way part of the cause for it. This can be hard to accept, but quite often the behavior of the boss is partly triggered by the behavior of the direct report. We saw this pattern in the intense exchanges between Doug and Warren in Chapter 5, where Doug felt micromanaged by Warren, but Warren felt he had to closely monitor because Doug provided too little information or opportunity to contribute. In response, Doug withheld even more.

This kind of reciprocal interchange is common enough that in any difficult situation it is worth considering. Is the boss who never has enough time for you partly avoiding you because once started, you go into extensive detail and never know when to stop? Is the boss who keeps you from making contacts outside the organization with important stakeholders you think could be helpful, and appears to be jealous, reacting to your way of showing off about your external status? How about the boss who criticizes you publicly and seems to want to embarrass you? Has it been impossible for you to ever admit there's anything you don't know?

None of this is meant to be a version of blame the victim. It is just that in interactive interpersonal relationships, there is seldom one side completely at fault. The idea, in fact, is to avoid blame and engage in collaborative problem solving. You can facilitate that by at least asking whether there is anything you do to stimulate the specific behavior that drives you crazy. This reduces defensiveness in the boss and makes it possible to explore what you can each do to get on to more productive grounds.

9. Accept Your Boss's Concerns as Legitimate

Your boss might be just as hesitant as you are to raise issues. One way to start to build a relationship is to legitimize talking about issues that might be difficult for the other person to bring up. Here is how Kate

Granso, a 2011 Stanford MBA, proceeded when she encountered a hostile attitude from her potential boss in a dream job:

> I worked for four years in Portland, Oregon at Nike, Inc. before going to Stanford. My summer internship in a retail merchandising role cemented my desire to become the general manager and decision maker of a business line. I was lucky enough to land a role on the dotcom merchandising team at a leading retailer, and quickly learned the levers I could pull to drive a dotcom business. It became clear to me that merchandising was, in fact, the path I would pursue for a full-time role post graduation. However, I had my sights set on a different type of role than the one I experienced during my internship—I wanted to work for a brick-and-mortar chain, to be the one calling the merchandising shots and owning the in-store experience.
>
> I maintained a good relationship with my boss from my summer internship, and she eventually reached out to me to see if I was still interested in a merchandising role. She knew that one of the VPs at the company was looking to fill a position, and offered to recommend me if I was interested. The one thing she warned against, however, was that most people were expected to start in the trenches and work their way up through the organization, so I might face some resistance—particularly as an MBA.
>
> I was able to secure an interview with the person my boss recommended. Our first meeting started off polite, but cool. She asked how I thought my experience at Stanford would help me in merchandising. I realized that was more of a (negative) statement than a question, so I tried to keep my defensiveness down. I decided to take the risk of trying to get at her underlying concern. "My guess is that you haven't had all positive experiences with MBAs?"
>
> Although I meant to sound curious (not accusatory), she did seem a little taken aback. "MBAs don't necessarily make good merchants; they often have a 'know-it-all' attitude," she said. I felt defensive, but I didn't want to react that way. I wanted to show that I valued my experiences, and that I thought that I could provide a lot to her organization.

I acknowledged her concerns about MBAs and asked her what some of her experiences had been with them. She said that some of the ones that she hired had carried their "MBA Badge" too proudly and thought they could be successful by only crunching data without doing the "dirty work" of reaching out to the stores for their input in business operations. "They apparently thought that was beneath them."

I continued to acknowledge her concern and then said how I could be different and bring a sense of curiosity to the role that's necessary to be a good merchant. The tone of the conversation took a complete 180 degree turn, as I think she suddenly realized that I may not be like every other MBA—and might instead be someone she could coach and mentor. She then asked more questions about my interests—questions that seemed as if she was really interested in me and not just trying to prove that I was like every other MBA.

Three days later, I received a call from her offering me the job I wanted.

10. Don't Undermine Yourself

Not everything goes as well as it did with Kate. Your boss likely has feelings about you, as you have about him or her. Launching this discussion might lead your boss to bring up a series of issues—and something that you initially thought would be a simple discussion suddenly leads to unanticipated revelations.

Watch Out for Alligators

Consider the analogy of wading through a swamp. You first try to find where the stones are to carefully step on, but the path eventually disappears. There are a series of (personal) alligators that can bite you. The first problem you may encounter is the tendency to too quickly retreat rather than press forward. "Sorry boss, not really a big deal." But you'll miss the opportunity to clear the air and restart the relationship with better mutual understanding.

Though this discussion won't be a straight line, you must focus on the distant shore of the desired partnership relationship. It is difficult to hear a series of criticisms and recriminations like, "If you only did your job, we wouldn't have any problems between us." The second alligator is responding defensively and beginning to engage in self-justification. Kate had to separate herself from MBAs in general; how will you react if your boss criticizes something that you did?

None of us wants to be blamed for something that isn't our fault, and we hate to be misunderstood. However, our impulse to set the record straight, can set off a pattern of mutual recriminations. "If you didn't keep changing priorities, we wouldn't have this problem." The third alligator is trying to determine—or worse, *prove*—who is right. Don't ignore the past; rather, use past events to determine what needs to be done to keep those problems from occurring in the future. The objective is to agree upon what each party needs to do to achieve the desired future.

The fourth alligator is failing to explore what really bothers your manager. In the discussion, your boss is likely to either explicitly or implicitly reveal his or her concerns. A general comment such as "If you deal with other areas, it's important not to lose sight of our area's needs" is the sort of statement that is easy to just agree with. But this risks missing an opportunity to understand what is *really* going on. What isn't your manager saying? Has this been a problem with others in the past—or is it specifically about you? Rather than just agreeing with his or her surface statement, can you use this opportunity to find out the underlying issue—as Kate did when her potential boss asked about how her two years at Stanford related to merchandising?

Remember—you are constantly keeping the partnership mindset. This isn't about you alone; you have to stay focused on what the boss needs and what is best for the organization. You also want to avoid the trap of increasing your boss's workload or failing to take on appropriate responsibility. For example, do you feel that your boss fails to give you the full picture of what is occurring? What can you do to inquire rather than passively waiting to be told? You want to be constantly working on responding as if you were a junior partner and not the powerless victim. For example, "I want to know the larger picture because I am the kind of person who totally commits and best delivers when I can see the whole."

You may not complete this discussion in one setting. You may reach an impasse and revisit the conversation at a later date. But your goal is to allow some reflection time—not retreat from the swamp.

There is a fifth alligator: depending on your boss to satisfy some of your needs. Listen closely to the complaints of Kevin Gerard about his boss, and you can probably see that this is as much about his own expectations as the boss's perhaps imperfect behavior:

> I'm beginning to think my problems with my boss have to do with a difference in style. I have certainly made a concerted effort to partner with him, but I sometimes wonder if he and my company are truly fulfilling my needs. While I really enjoy the work I do, I am sometimes uninspired by the environment and culture.
>
> My boss is usually very direct about business matters, but isn't when it comes to personal matters. For example, he doesn't tell someone when he doesn't like them; instead, he talks about them behind their backs. He only gives praise in the form of public announcements (e.g., awards ceremonies with plaques and photos). This makes it hard to tell where you stand with him on a day-to-day basis. Interestingly enough, that is also how *his* boss operates.
>
> One of the things that gets my juices flowing is feeling on top of my game—being confident, informed, and generally good at what I do. However, I've often felt ill-prepared and tentative in my current role. One of the "problems" is that I was elevated into a role two weeks after I started my job. At first, I felt challenged by this "stretch" assignment, but it's particularly uncomfortable to be in this role in a company in which you're expected to start from the bottom and earn your promotions. The times I've tried to solicit help, the people to whom I've reached out haven't been particularly warm or helpful. I don't necessarily think they *don't* want me to succeed, but I certainly don't think any of them take it upon themselves to lend a helping hand.

I don't think I've been set up for success in my role, and it often seems like trial by fire. I worry about falling flat on my face. I need words of affirmation, or at least some feedback—I have felt completely in the dark about my performance since I started. On the one hand, I need to show my boss that I'm up for the challenge, but on the other hand, since I've heard my boss snicker about people behind their backs, I constantly assume that he thinks the same things about me and just isn't telling me.

I have friends both inside and outside the organization who can support me here. At the same time, I still seek affirmation from my boss, even if I get it from friends, family, and even other coworkers. Last week my boss stopped by my desk to thank me for some work I had done for a senior leadership meeting—it felt really good, and afterwards one of my coworkers told me that it was "cool" that he had done so, because he almost never thanks anyone for their work. Even that little nugget was enough to reinforce that the effort I put into our work was validated, and gave me the motivation to keep it up.

Perhaps what I am getting caught up with is whether or not the effort is even worth it—if not, shouldn't I spend my time doing something that is worth it?

Kevin isn't in an easy situation. He has been given an assignment that is a real stretch for him and he legitimately wonders, as anyone might, "Can I really do this?" But these are the crucible assignments that cause growth and provide the opportunity to demonstrate, or discover, valuable competencies. He is also in an organization where praise is incredibly rare—and therefore highly valuable. This may not be the best climate for individual development, but it is what it is. It is also a culture where asking for affirmation from the boss might well be seen as a sign of weakness.

Kevin is getting some affirmation not just from friends, but also from coworkers and every so often from his boss. Yet by his constant seeking approval, he is allowing his motivational level to be determined by his boss. Kevin wants something that his boss is not comfortable giving, but whose problem is that? It's an alligator he could keep caged.

Reaching Agreement

When the relationship is strained and/or the conversation is difficult, many organizational members retreat to generalities and get out of the meeting as soon as possible. The danger is moving to toothless conclusions such as, "I will keep you informed" (about *what* and *how often?*) or "We should meet more often" (*How often* and *who calls the meetings?*). That is the sixth alligator: failing to talk specifically about what *each is going to do*. In fact, generalities can be worse than not having raised the issue in the first place. Hard feelings are sure to arise if each person leaves the meeting with a different understanding of what should come next. Then when expectations cross, each silently says some variation of, "I knew that I couldn't trust that glib talker." Repairing that conclusion is even more difficult than having the discussion in the first place.

The junior partner must constantly be aware of what you can take on when working out agreements. Is the issue that your boss doesn't always pass on information that he acquires from *his* boss? Why not ask him after those meetings, "Did anything go on that would be useful for me to know about?" Chances are that your boss's superior often changes priorities; so you might broach this subject by saying, "I realize that I assume that each priority is set in stone when that might not be the case. I am going to start checking with you how 'firm' you think that direction is. Also, when I hear through the grapevine that some things might be changing, I am going to take the initiative to check with you rather than waiting. Is that alright with you?"

Sometimes it is necessary to set up interim experiments. "Let's try, for the next two months, to meet every Monday morning at 8:30 to review the upcoming week and see if that is enough." Be certain that a deadline is set (and met) to review this agreement.

Even the most thorough discussion holds the danger that each party will walk away with slightly different understandings of what they agreed to do next. Again, we are putting the responsibility on you, the junior partner, to go back and send a confirming memo, "I want to make sure that I have it correct about what we decided. I think it was A, B, and C."

If your boss is willing, it can be useful for you to meet with her for even 15 minutes a day or so later to see how she's feeling. This will allow you to discuss any second thoughts, and to see how your boss feels about this sort of conversation. For example—is it alright to discuss "how we are dealing with each other" or is that too touchy-feely for him or her? (This is a case that we cover in the next chapter).

Follow-Through and Handling Regression

The proof of any agreement is in the subsequent action. You as junior partner must come through on agreements, and handle them productively when your boss doesn't. The last alligator is to sit back and build negative explanations for your boss's backsliding behavior. This is the time to get curious. "I wonder why a well-intentioned person would act this way?" If you can keep that nonaccusatory mind-set, then it is possible to approach your boss with a question about apparent failure to stick to the agreement.

The ensuing conversation might produce an apology (and hopefully a deeper commitment on your boss's part because you are expecting accountability), or it could give you a deeper understanding of the situation that your boss is in. Have you made the assumption that your boss is in total control of his calendar only to find out how much uncertainty is produced by *his* boss?

If there are repeated violations, then it might be necessary to raise the ante. We cover how to do that in the next two chapters.

8

The Art—and Responsibility—of Helping Your Boss Succeed

As a junior partner, there are many payoffs to helping your boss succeed:

- It increases the chance of the unit/organization being successful (because there are at least two of you on the task).
- You grow your competencies as you take on more challenging work.
- It means that your boss is more likely to move on to newer and better things, opening up the possibility for you to do the same.
- You build a "line of credit" that you can use to allow you to have the opportunities and autonomy to be successful.

- You develop a reputation for being committed to more than personal advancement—which has a positive effect outside your area.

Helping your boss implies that you have influence—and direct reports usually have more influence than they first think, because they command more currencies than they realize. There are many things that your manager needs from you. In addition to performing your assigned responsibilities, you can be the source of new ideas, take initiative to resolve problems before they grow, be a sounding board, and recognize new opportunities.

Taking on Some of the Boss's Tasks

Decisions are made too high in the hierarchy in most organizations. One reason is that managers bring along the tasks they are comfortable with at a lower position as they climb onto the next rung on the ladder. Although these tasks may be easy to complete, they lack the excitement and growth that would occur if someone one or two levels down completed them.

We have tested this numerous times in our work with management teams in what we call the "Hospital Experiment." We say to the assembled team: "Imagine that your manager is quite sick and can't be disturbed for the next seven months. Though he will recover and come back, the company doesn't plan on replacing him in the meantime. Instead, you, collectively, must divide up his work, with individuals taking on the tasks that they think they can perform at a satisfactory level."

Three things happen:

1. The team members jump into this assignment and decide that they, collectively, can usually take on between 60 percent and 80 percent of the boss's job. They also say that it is more exciting than the work they are presently doing.

2. The boss—who observes this—looks increasingly worried. He eventually admits, "I have some concerns. Mike wants to represent me on that task force, but he might push his own area and fail to take account of the entire department. And Maria wants to handle some time-sensitive assignments, but she has a tendency to submit things late." (The direct reports often respond, "But why haven't you told us this before?" That opens considerable discussion and much-needed feedback.)

3. The manager still looks troubled after the air has cleared. He finally blurts out, "But if you take on that much, what is my job?" The others respond, "Your key job is dealing upward and sideways with upper management and with other divisions, not wasting your time with things that we can do."

The moral of this exercise is that one of the ways that junior partners can help their manager is to look over what the boss does and ask the question, "Are some of these tasks that I could do? Would it be a growth experience for me while taking some of the load off my boss's shoulders?" And that is the way you can frame this topic when talking with your manager. It may be that you are especially good at or interested in an activity that your boss doesn't like—thereby making the situation a win-win.

You might wonder, "Why should I take on additional work when I am already overloaded?" But in a partnership orientation, what is sauce for the goose is sauce for the gander. Wouldn't you want your direct reports to also partner with you? What could *they* do that would offload tasks from you—and let you do the same with your boss?

Relieving the Boss of Heroic Tendencies

Most leaders tend to feel overly responsible for their unit's management and overall success. This prompts direct reports to assume that they are responsible only for their areas and that it's the boss's job to take care of the larger issues.[1] Yet performance and satisfaction grow substantially when employees undertake "shared responsibility." And that can produce conditions of true partnership.

Leaders who take the traditional heroic approach tend to think they must have all the answers and can't ask for help. They worry that not having answers shows "weakness" and will cause direct reports to think less of them. However, showing this kind of vulnerability in aspects that aren't critical to the leader's core competence can show one's humanness—and can *increase* acceptance.

David saw this vividly in working with a family-owned company. Bill, the present chief executive officer (CEO), had taken over from his father five years before. When Bill's father died, company executives attended the large funeral ceremony. Just before starting the next Executive Committee meeting, the vice presidents told Bill how touched they were at the event. Although Bill seemed pleased, he started the meeting by reviewing the agenda. David stopped him and asked with considerable emotion, "Bill, your father, who built this company, is no longer here. How does it feel now having all the responsibility?" The room went silent as Bill started to talk about the range of feelings he had, not only of grief, but also the burden of carrying on the legacy. The 10 minutes of genuine response not only enhanced the members' respect for Bill; it significantly increased the team's cohesion and commitment to the company.

You don't need such an extreme situation to encourage your boss to show his or her humanness. It may be nothing more than "giving permission" to lay aside that heroic mental model: "You don't need to have all the answers. You can use us to join with you to find the answer." Or, "You seem worried and concerned. But you aren't sharing that with us. What's upsetting you?" It might be an informal conversation in which you mention that *you* don't have heroic expectations of her and would actually respect her if she wanted to ask for help. Of course, this requires that you lay aside your heroic wish to have the perfect boss and can accept her humanity—limitations as well as strengths.

Proactively Giving Support

Whether the leader heads the entire organization or a division, it can indeed be lonely at the top. Part of this is the heroic isolation of not being able to share concerns, doubts, or the desire to ask for help. Another is not feeling understood or appreciated for all the effort that goes with the role.

You also want to support any changes your manager is trying to produce. For example, perhaps he is under pressure from top management to cut costs. In addition to cooperating in your area, how do you respond to colleagues who complain about the boss pushing this program? Do you join in on the griping or explain the situation the boss is in? Is there any way you can help? Partnering isn't blind acceptance of everything your manager does. If, in a particular situation, you don't agree with how he is going about the cost-cutting, that has to be directly addressed with your manager: "In order to defend this new directive to others, I need to fully understand why we are going about it this way because I think it is causing some unnecessary resistance."

Leaders often need support as well in articulating their vision—the personal dream that leaders have for their area. These dreams are often deeply buried within the individual and tend to be expressed in a dry, impersonal manner when they are brought out. Leadership is not only about having a vision; it also requires the ability to express to others what that vision means personally.

The junior partner can help by asking the boss about his or her personal vision for this unit. Your boss is giving a certain number of years to this job; what personal value does it hold for him or her? And how can you help him express that to others?

Knowing the Impact of Your Boss's Behavior

Another currency you often hold is your view of some of the unintended consequences of your manager's actions. After giving a talk on influence at a conference, an executive came up to David and confessed:

> I blew it with my last boss. I was on a six-month assignment with the director of marketing and we quickly built a good working relationship—in spite of some things that he did. Though he wasn't entirely dishonest, he had a tendency to tell people what they wanted to hear. I could read him rather well so it didn't bother me as much as it bothered others.
>
> He regularly came into my office to complain; "I don't know why other areas don't trust us—it really makes our work so much more difficult." I knew exactly what he did that caused this mistrust, but rather than telling him, I just commiserated with him. I now see how I lost an opportunity to really be a partner.

Leaders often complain about what is going on: "Why are people going in different directions when I clearly laid out the strategic vision?" "Why did this misguided product plan happen when I have stressed that we need to be close to the customers?" "The economy is in the dumps; people should know that we have to cut costs." When the problem is only technical, direct reports are more likely to speak up: "We need to change the way employees account for costs." But they are more likely to hold back when the issue involves the leader's behavior. Even though that might appear to be the prudent response, it limits both the boss and the organization's success. But how can one raise issues that involve the manager's behavior without stepping into a career-limiting move?

Helping Your Boss Be a Better Boss

Who better knows how a leader leads than those whom he or she leads? Direct reports know whether the boss runs meetings that are useful or counterproductive. They know whether the boss creates clarity or confusion when talking about the organization's direction. And they know what he does that encourages or discourages taking initiative. Yet, direct reports who think of giving feedback to their superiors fear being considered presumptuous. Honest feedback may be offered when there is a crisis (and a consultant is brought in) or when the employee is quite skilled or close to his or her boss. But because junior partners need to be committed to their manager's success, there are ways they can help the manager improve even when the relationship isn't fully developed. In fact, assisting in this way can help build toward deeper partnership.

Because most people take their strengths for granted, one way to show support is to point out these easily overlooked talents. "Boss, I admire the way you kept from getting defensive when challenged." "You really have a talent for pulling together the best points of different peoples' arguments." "I am learning from you to let conflict develop rather than trying to prematurely shut it down."

Junior partners often fear being seen as "brown-nosing" and therefore hold back. Our experience is that it's fairly obvious when someone says something complimentary solely for the sake of ingratiation. For example, upper-level managers in a large company talked about the tactics of a third colleague: "Jim believes that people like flattery and whenever he tells me something nice, I cut it in half." His colleague laughed and said, "I cut it to one-fourth." Then they mentioned another executive. "Dan's comments I can trust. Not only does he seem to mean it, but he also tells me when I do screw up."

Flattery is to ingratiate; positive feedback is to help others become more aware of their strengths. You also want to be specific both about what is valuable in their present behavior as well as areas for development. However, it's best to separate these in time, because each has value in its own right. We talked in Chapter 5 about the limits of the "sandwich" feedback technique, in which you start with a positive, slip in the critical, and end with a positive. Not only does this not fool anybody, but it devalues the positive.

Employees have trouble giving authentic positive comments, but they also tend to hold back potentially developmental feedback, or raise issues in a way that is either ineffective or counterproductive. We see this repeatedly in an exercise in our leadership programs dealing with "Partnering with Your Boss." There is a case involving John, the regional director of marketing, and his direct reports. They are meeting to decide whether to spend money on local, regional, or national trade shows. The participants watch a video of the meeting where Craig, one of the direct reports, presents his report and strongly pushes for national trade shows. John disagrees with Craig's recommendation, "but he doesn't want to demotivate Craig" by being overt about preferring regional. Instead, he uses leading questions to call on the other direct reports, elicit the information he wants, and then steer them in the "right" direction. Though Craig tries to counter, he's met with more questions that John directs to the other members. In the end, John is able to say, "It looks like regional trade shows are the best option"—and all the members, except Craig, nod in dutiful agreement.

We then set up a role-play where one of us acts as John, and the participants act as a direct report other than Craig. They are to discuss with John how to be a better boss. Participants are briefed that John sees himself as a "modern manager" who believes in collaborative decision making. However, people have heard him complain that his team isn't operating as well as it should. He also has an open-door policy, so is quite approachable.

This should be an easy assignment. The junior partners not only know John's goals, but can accept them. They also know firsthand the effect of John's behavior and the ways that it is keeping him from achieving these objectives. Finally, John is accessible and is neither punitive nor defensive—as long as he doesn't feel attacked.

In playing our role as John, we are neither resistant nor punitive, but have a bit of a "tin ear." We don't pick up on hints or indirect statements, but only respond if the junior partner is direct without being antagonistic.

Their job is to role-play giving John "developmental" feedback. This shouldn't be difficult, yet, almost inevitably, each participant playing a direct report acts in an ineffectual way and subsequently loses influence. Many start off by trying to "sweet-talk" John, telling him what a great boss he is. But rather than getting him to be more receptive, this style tends to produce mistrust as John senses insincerity and wonders, "What the hell are they up to?"

The direct report then follows up with an oblique comment or a pseudo-question. "John, do you think yesterday's meeting went well?"

Now, if John was perceptive, he might sense that the question wasn't really a question and respond, "Do you have some concerns, Norm?" But, as we said, John has a "tin ear" and takes the question at face value. "Yes, I thought we came up with a good decision." And the person playing the subordinate gives up.

We then have others try, who decide to "up the ante" and—assuming that they're being "direct"—make accusatory comments that imply that John has negative intentions. "John, you had clearly made up your mind before the meeting and were just trying to manipulate us." Such interpretive attributions create the exact defensiveness that the direct report was worried about.

So what's the alternative to this approach? Think of the concepts that we have covered: (1) Start by assuming that your boss is acting reasonably from his or her point of view; (2) realize that your expertise is that you know whether the boss's behavior is meeting his or her goals, especially with you; (3) find the goal that you can support even though you disagree on the means; and (4) join with your boss and make it an issue of *we* not *you*. With those principles in mind, here is a composite of how several conversations have unfolded:

> "John, do you have 20 minutes to talk about yesterday's meeting? I don't think it went as well as either of us would have liked."

> [John] "Sure, but I thought that we arrived at the correct decision."

> "We might have, but that is not what I came to talk about. I think what you want—and certainly what I want—is a meeting where everybody speaks up and talks straight to each other, and I don't think we did that."

> [John] "You have a point there. People were sitting on their hands. That is why I called on people; I think that helped, don't you?"

> "No, I don't think so. While I appreciate your attempts to help, it actually took the responsibility off of us. Also, your questions were heard as leading us to a certain outcome, and we took the easy route and agreed with you."

[**John**] "Well what do you suggest? (*At this point, we can begin to implement the partnership of joint problem solving.*)

Before sharing with participants what this alternative might look like, we ask them, "How would you want your direct reports to raise an issue with you when they have trouble with your approach?" Almost to a person they say, "Be direct. Don't beat around the bush. Tell it like it is." What is so fascinating is that experienced executives want the unvarnished truth from their direct reports, but have difficulty giving it to their bosses.

This is not to say that every attempt has failed in this exercise. In fact, one of the better responses was the following:

(*The direct report walks into John's office*). "John, I want to talk to you about yesterday's meeting; I think we let you down."

[**John, surprised**] "What do you mean?"

"I think we would agree that it is important that all the issues be on the table—good news as well as bad." [John nods]. "However, we are relying on you to bring out the bad news and in so doing, we aren't carrying out our responsibility. We are in this negative loop where, because you ask us questions to surface our doubts, we don't initiate—and because we don't initiate, you ask. That's not the team we want or think we can have."

[**John**] "So what do you suggest?"

"I will talk with my peers, but if you just open up the meeting by asking for the main issues and concerns—without posing what appear to be leading questions—we will raise our concerns. Would that work for you?"

Note the exchange qualities in this interaction. The first one reveals a negative exchange (the more John probes for problems, the less direct reports initiate, which gets John to probe further). And the second one is an agreement with the boss ("if we do X, will you not do Y?"). Furthermore, there is a strong partnership orientation: the direct report owns his part of the problem rather than just blaming John and initiates a mutually beneficial solution.

Because the preceding interactions might seem a bit too pat, let's complicate things. What if the boss asks halfway through the discussion, "Why the hell didn't you raise this in the meeting?" Again, this would be a great opportunity to negotiate for the future if you can keep from becoming defensive.

"I am sorry, John. I should have, and I let you down. I just wasn't sure if I could raise this in front of the others. I didn't want you to feel put on the spot or that I was disloyal. How do you want me to handle this in the future?"

The situation might be further worsened if you sense that John is getting defensive and sending signals that you read as disapproving. This might be a time to take it up a level—which might go like this:

"John, you seem bothered that I am raising this issue. I want the sort of relationship where I don't have to hold back or be indirect. My intention is to be helpful. If I have some ideas about how our team can work better together, I would like to raise it. Am I doing anything that is causing a problem?"

Many managers are concerned about whether their direct reports are giving them "the whole truth." So in a sense, talking about building conditions where you don't have to hold back is in both your and your boss's best interests. If you are interested in going deeper into how to conduct this kind of dialogue, see Appendix A, "Power Talk: A Hands-On Guide to Supportive Confrontation," in our previous book *Power Up: Transforming Organizations through Shared Leadership.*

For Whose Sake?

Even though we strongly believe that it is a junior partner's responsibility to help the boss be a better boss, there are some words of warning. First, don't think that you can shape the "perfect boss" to get exactly what you want with enough feedback. There are limits to how much any individual can (or wants to) change. For example, Jack is an executive we worked with who hated conflict. No matter how much input he received, it was still difficult for him when things got hot in meetings. But his direct reports made an agreement with him; whenever he would try to deflect or put off a disagreement, they would laugh and kiddingly say, "come on, Jack, we can deal with this." You must accept that we all have limits; longing for your manager to change in ways that are near impossible might move you from being a junior partner to being a major nuisance.

Additionally, some very powerful bosses have armored themselves against the possibility of hearing certain kinds of disconfirming feedback. Again we turn to the experiences of someone who has made a career out of speaking truth to power—Len Schlesinger, who has been the direct report to powerful people in both business (The Limited and Au Bon Pain) and academia (Harvard Business School, Ohio State, and Brown), as well as a researcher who has studied many executives:

> As soon as powerful people like successful entrepreneurs get a taste of power, they rewrite their own life history. That excludes many below from the belief that they can take action. I call it the "as told to" school of entrepreneurship; they come to believe their own story because it is written. The powerful tell themselves stories about their successes and skills in a self-reinforcing dynamic that edits out messages that don't fit the story.

In other words, even when you do all the right things to give feedback as a junior partner, you may not be able to get through. And yet, sometimes—as with Mr. Menon and Mollie, from Chapter 2—it is possible to penetrate the resistance, in the interests of helping the organization become more effective.

So how do you know what to bring up? Listen carefully to complaints and concerns your boss expresses. As we mentioned earlier, most leaders are quite vocal about the things that dissatisfy them and direct reports often know what the boss is doing—or *not* doing—that is causing the problem. You probably have a boatload of expressed currencies to which you can tie your feedback. See your manager's complaints as expressing currencies in which he or she would be relieved to have you pay. When feedback comes with a partnership orientation, it is not a criticism—but rather, a gift. Joel Peterson, chairman of the board of JetBlue, repeatedly says, "Feedback is the Breakfast of Champions."

CHAPTER

9

Recovering from Failed Talks with Your Boss

The previous chapter showed you that—even with the occasional difficult moment—*it is possible* to launch a new, more satisfying relationship with your boss. But what if these efforts *don't* work? What if, when you tried to give your boss feedback, he or she hit you with one of these power-oriented shots:

- Look, I'm the boss and I don't need you to tell me what to do.
- If you just did your job, we wouldn't have any problems.
- Are you questioning my authority?
- This all sounds nice, but you really don't understand the situation.
- If I wanted your opinion, I would have asked for it.

You might either argue back or worry that you're on thin ice and get out of there as soon as possible—and maybe even start polishing your resume. But what about a third alternative: addressing the differing expectations directly to alter them? We'll explain exactly how to do this here.

First, retreat from the heat of the interaction to quickly ask yourself whether you've possibly done something to create this resistance. After all, you have more influence over yourself than over your boss—so start where you can most easily control the outcome! Might you be doing any of the following?

Ways You Might Have Trapped Yourself

- Not fully sharing your intentions—causing your boss to suspect your motives.
- Not aligning with common goals.
- Talking about your desires in a way that implies you think your boss is inadequate, a failure, a jerk.
- Not speaking to your manager's needs or concerns.
- Increasing your boss's workload; shifting responsibility upward.

If you aren't doing any of this, the next step is to monitor your mind-set. Instead of making negative attributions about the boss, consider that "my boss is acting reasonably from his/her point of view"—no matter how unreasonable the behavior appears to be. It helps to come up with at least two reasonable alternative explanations for your boss's behavior. Here is a starter list:

- He is getting pressure from his boss.
- She is more worried about the long-term (or short-term) effect.
- There is an unannounced big strategic move about to happen.
- In a previous job, that action worked well.
- She wants to demonstrate her competence.
- He feels uncomfortable with uncertainty and is asserting his view to feel better.

You can think of the actual causes once you let go of the automatic assumption that the boss is "unreasonable."

Is there any way for you to see these "attacks" as concerns your manager is conveying—and therefore potential opportunities? Can you find a way to "pay" your boss by giving him or her what they care about? Instead of defending against the attack, hear it as a painful manifestation of your boss's concerns, what is valued—his or her currencies. Pay by addressing or meeting those concerns rather than trying to get your boss to see the world exactly as you do.

This isn't an easy endeavor. You have taken the risk of raising an important topic that your boss is resisting—perhaps even making negative assertions about your intentions or performance. It is difficult in those circumstances to keep your defensiveness down, not start justifying yourself, and instead begin asking questions. But if it were easy, there would be no need for this book.

Can We Discuss the Way We Can Talk?

Partners should be able to bring major issues—both professional and personal—to the surface and directly deal with them. However, people have their own preferred way of dealing with issues. For example, does your boss expect you to:

- Always come with a solution and not just the problem?
- Offer your entire analysis before conclusions, or vice versa?
- Always bring a careful financial analysis, or can you start discussions with your hunches?

In terms of interpersonal style:

- How direct can you be with that particular boss?
- How do you both handle disagreements?

- How much leeway are you both comfortable with?
- How does he or she treat mistakes?

In previous eras, the boss's style automatically determined the rules of the game, and subordinates conformed or suffered the consequences. However, partnership allows you to mutually work out the "rules" of interaction.

For example, here is how George Temke, a middle-level manufacturing executive in an international organization, handles shaping the relationship from below:

> I make sure, before accepting a job, that my new boss understands my aspirations and the type of relationship that I hope we will have. I emphasize the fact that I would like to know if he isn't pleased with my work or the way that I do my job. I don't like surprises in this area. Once this has been established, I do not remember having to bring it up again. I find that there is a degree of mutual respect that exists and tends to carry over as the relationship develops.

Sometimes a boss will overtly challenge you and ask whether you are questioning authority. More often, however, you pick up cues of displeasure—the furrowed brow or slightly sharper tone of voice. It is tempting either to push harder to convince your boss that you are only trying to help, or to mumble an apology and back off. But instead of taking either of these tactics, consider stopping the conversation on the work task level, and asking to talk about "how we are talking":

"Let's pause for a moment; I am concerned about the way we are interacting. First, I want to be clear that I certainly don't mean to attack you or your right to make the decisions. You're in charge. I just want to improve our interaction so we get great results. To do that, I want to feel free to put important and difficult stuff on the table, but it appears to me that you aren't happy with my raising this hot potato. Is that right?"

Irrespective of how the boss responds, you could add:

"I don't think it serves either of us well for me to be silent on potentially controversial or upsetting issues. However, do I bring them up in a way that bothers you? I want to figure that out together. How can I be honest with you without giving the impression that I am not on your side?"

The objective is to find a way of interacting that makes the issues clear and leads to joint problem solving. But it has to take both individuals' styles into account.

This conversation doesn't have to occur when there is an undercurrent of displeasure. It doesn't hurt to check in to see how the boss is reacting to your approach—and it can be as easy as saying something like:

"I don't know how this discussion we have just had struck you. Although it hasn't been easy for me, I'm pleased because I feel free to directly raise everything and not beat around the bush. But I want to voice both of our concerns—so is there anything that you think I should do differently?"

This approach lets you discuss *ways you are working* together, and makes it clear that you are both on the same team. If you can talk about disagreements at this level, you become better able to resolve conflicts (and therefore, act like a partner). You're not trying to outsmart your boss; you just want to join forces with him.

Note as well that the language we use in these conversations is business-like work process, not soft and squishy. If you work in a culture where everyone talks comfortably about feelings, then by all means— let your emotions fly. However, this approach is appropriate in a more buttoned-up culture. (For an example of dangers in this touchy territory, see the example of Andy and Gwen later in the chapter.)

Disagreeing with Your Boss . . . and Surviving or Thriving

We commonly hear the anxious question, "How can I disagree with my boss without endangering the relationship?" Junior partners worry that managers will see them as an obstacle, and not a team player. Although there are some bosses with whom you can't disagree, those cases are rarer than most people think. The major problem is *how* the disagreement is handled.

However, no matter what the case, we insist on one absolute rule: No matter how strongly you disagree with your boss about an issue, you must *never* challenge your boss's right to override you. Formal organizations grant all managers this right—whether or not their judgment is correct in each case. You can challenge the data, the reasoning, and the decision—but do not challenge formal authority.

When he or she agrees with the boss, the direct report usually makes declarative statements and moves closer (psychologically and even physically): "Jim, I think this memo is an excellent idea." But when disagreeing, the direct report uses a cautious tone and gives an opinion as a question: "Do you really think presenting it that way will work?" The employee actually means, "I don't agree that the memo as written will work, but I am too worried about your reaction to say that directly."

Not only is this a low-power statement on the direct report's part, but it actually can make the boss suspicious ("I wonder what he is really saying?"). At worst, the manager takes the statement at face value and answers by saying, "Yes, I think that presentation will knock them out." The employee goes quiet, saying to himself, "Sure glad that I was indirect—look at how adamant the boss was," without realizing that his pseudo-question actually *caused* that response.

Goals or Means?

The crucial distinction here is not between the safety of *agreeing* or the riskiness of *disagreeing*—but whether the disagreement is about basic *goals* or the best *means* to achieve commonly agreed upon goals. Most disagreements in organizations are about means or methods. For example—both you and your boss want to increase market share, but disagree on how to achieve it. If that is the case, you can directly (and powerfully) disagree by being on the boss's side on goals, even though you disagree about means. "Mike, I also think it is imperative that we get people focused on market share, but I am afraid that the wording in this memo will be confusing to some. Can we take a look at this?" That way you aren't moving away from the boss; you're joining in what is really important.

The other distinction is the way you respond if the manager still resists. Keep in mind that one of your tasks as a junior partner is to make sure the boss doesn't make a big mistake. "Sorry, Mike, but I can't let this drop. Increasing market share is one of our core metrics and I am also committed to achieving that." Of course, a responsible junior partner doesn't just increase the boss's workload, so might add, "I might be wrong, but let me check with a couple of my contacts in the field and try my hand at redrafting this; you have enough on your plate." Sometimes there comes a point where even the most committed junior partner gives way. In organizations like Intel that value disagreement, the norm is "dissent and then commit." But with even frustrated partnership attempts, the point at which budding partners back down is later than has historically been the case in the traditional superior-subordinate relationship.

When You Can't Accept the Goals

Of course, it only works if you *do* agree on the goals. But what if that is not the case; what if you can't accept your boss's goals? What if your manager, in meetings with people from other departments, cuts them down with bullying and scorn—and tells you afterward, "It's important to show them that I am not to be fooled with." She emphasizes how critical it is to make sure that the department's goals are primary.

Before you completely give up, you need to look under the hood. Your boss has a sequence of three goals. You might not buy into the first two—helping her appear tough and immovable—but can't you join with the third—achieving your department's objectives—and say something like: "I agree that we need to make sure we achieve our departmental objectives—and we need others' cooperation to do so. I am concerned that we might be building unnecessary resistance. Can we talk about how we can show our determination to others without making them feel antagonized?"

Keep in mind that many goals are simply *means* to more basic goals. The objective is to find a goal that you can accept and partner on with your boss. And if there are fundamental differences on core goals, you may need to consider whether this is the organization to which you can commit.

Standing Up to a Powerhouse

The discussion so far can sound as if you have to turn yourself in knots and watch every word in order to disagree with your boss. However, there's a big difference between identifying true goals and playing amateur psychologist. We offer the following example to demonstrate that it is possible to push back. Although the person in the example is a consultant—and therefore not totally dependent on keeping this job—it was an extremely desirable one. You can judge for yourself.

The powerhouse boss involved was former General Electric chief executive officer (CEO) and well-known confrontational executive Jack Welch. Welch's power and influence have been well documented by many, and there's plenty of evidence to suggest that Welch is not an easy person to push back on—even for a nervy consultant.

But lead consultant Len Schlesinger did it. Len had been assigned to work with NBC on the GE Work Out program. Welch hated a video that NBC had made for Work Out about the cumbersome process of expense reimbursement. Though it had been staged like a *Saturday Night Live* sketch and was hilarious, Welch felt that Work Out should be about organizational transformation and a cultural revolution, and that the video trivialized a simple work process. Right after it was shown to all the Work Out consultants, Welch declared that it should be "collected and destroyed and never shown again."

As Len tells it:

> Jack was standing next to me at a break in the men's room when I told him I loved the movie and will use it again. I let him know that we had to empower the GE work force by making sure their basic needs were met. As soon as I explained why and how I wanted to

use the video, Welch completely reversed his position and suggested that we debate the issue with the other consultants. My colleagues thought I was crazy, but as I saw it, I had nothing to lose;
he already said he didn't like my work, so at worst, I was finished.
What's so terrible about fighting back? And the final decision was
to use it.

It can be easier to take such a calculated risk if you think in
advance about the worst thing that could happen as a result of your
action. The premortem is a really useful device: assess the worst possible consequence and plan for it; if you are willing to pay that price,
then risk recedes, because you have decided *a priori* that you are willing
to pay. And keep in mind that things seldom turn out as badly as you
imagine them in advance.

With luck, you may never have to deal with as powerful a boss
as Jack Welch, although those who stand up to powerful bosses often
earn considerable respect. Fit between boss and junior partner matters.

But What If Directness Does Not Work?
Andy's Vanishing Boss

What to do when the approaches we've already covered don't work?
Take the situation of Andy Warren, a middle-level manager in an international corporation. When Andy checked his e-mail on Sunday night,
he was shocked to see that his boss, Gwen, had not responded to the
e-mail he had sent her on Friday afternoon.

Ten months before, Andy had just started the job and worked for
a manager named Cathy. Cathy was an empowering and collaborative boss who encouraged the partnership that Andy wanted. However,
Cathy moved to another division and was replaced by Gwen, a British
accountant and former controller.

Andy was disappointed with how things were going from the
very start of their relationship. Despite his best attempts to give
her the benefit of the doubt, Gwen seemed to be micromanaging,

manipulative, and dishonest. She left Andy out of meetings that he and others assumed he would be a part of. She waited until five minutes before the end of a meeting to surface significant issues or change an important decision. And she scheduled meetings with Andy's direct reports without telling him. Though he requested that Gwen not do this anymore—and Gwen agreed—she met with two of his people several hours after he made this request.

Just this week, Gwen had pulled one of her usual moves. The group made a decision, and Gwen announced at the meeting's end that she was going to reverse it—despite the fact that it was one of the most thoughtful, time-consuming decisions Andy's team had ever made. He had had enough. His team was exasperated and looking to him to do something.

The easiest thing to do would have been to tell Gwen's boss, the chief financial officer, about the problems. However, Andy avoided doing this because he worried it would create a permanent rift between him and Gwen. When he went to Gwen's office to talk with her, he found that she had left for the weekend—so Andy wrote an e-mail titled "Reflections." He wrote: "I have spent some time reflecting on the meeting and see that it is not the decision you made that is troubling but the context of our working relationship. Over the past months I have felt distrusted and disempowered."

He went on to provide three specific incidents that led him to feel this way. He ended the e-mail with, "I am sorry to have sent this over e-mail rather than talking in person. I would love to meet first thing on Monday and wanted to let you know where I am so that we can have a productive meeting."

Despite the fact that Gwen answered just about every e-mail within 20 to 30 minutes, she still hadn't answered by Sunday night. All Andy could think about was the conversation he would have with Gwen the next day.

Andy had decided not to prejudge Gwen on Monday morning. Maybe she wanted to talk in person and did not want to put anything in writing over e-mail. However, that day Gwen ignored him despite his attempts to reach her via phone, e-mail, and stopping by her office. He kept trying to ping her on their internal system and would get no response. Finally, at 7:30 p.m. she called him on his cell phone.

All Gwen would address was the decision she'd made at the meeting; she would not talk about their relationship. Andy did not want her to think she was fixing the problem, so he decided to push a little harder. Even after using countless "I" statements and talking about her actions as not being aligned with her goals, Gwen would not hear anything. She kept saying, "This is clearly a miscommunication." Andy mentioned specifics and asked that she respect his style of managing. But he was getting nowhere. She made the same hollow promises that she had made before, but Andy was convinced that nothing was going to change. Frustrated and seriously thinking of quitting, Andy hung up the phone.

His assumptions were right. Nothing changed. Gwen kept meeting with his reports, not including him in meetings, and reversing key decisions at the last moment.

What is going on here? Is the conclusion that Gwen is impossible and/or that the approaches that we have discussed don't work? On the surface, it looks as if Andy has done everything that we suggested. He didn't start off by demonizing her, but kept seeing her as a potential partner; he directly raised the issue in a nonaccusatory way; and he pointed to specific examples rather than talking in generalities. When that didn't work, he wanted to talk about what might be problematic in how they were communicating. Aren't these all things that we have suggested?

Even though it contains aspects of our influence model, Andy violates three critical components. Let's review the steps in the model so we can link them with Andy's actions:

- Seeing the other as a potential partner
- Assessing the boss's power and the power gap
- Understanding the boss's world and identifying possible currencies
- Clarifying your priorities

- Relating to your boss as he or she prefers
- Negotiating win-win exchanges

Andy completed the first and second steps well. However, he dropped the ball during the third step, as he made little effort to understand Gwen's world. It wouldn't have taken much detective work on his part to discover that this was a rotation assignment on her part. He was aware that she followed a very popular leader, which had to be challenging for her. Therefore, she probably wanted a lot of information and did not feel comfortable trusting others' decisions.

Additional, Andy ran into some trouble clarifying his priorities (step four). It makes sense that he wants to be involved in decisions and not have them reversed at the last minute. But why was he so bothered that Gwen talked to his direct reports? She didn't seem to be turning them against Andy in any way.

The main problem is the way Andy chose to relate to Gwen (step five). He approached her in ways with which *he* was comfortable—talking about their relationship. Though it is important not to engage in stereotypes, it isn't wild speculation to say that neither the English nor accountants are known for feeling comfortable in these emotional domains. Andy should have quickly sensed this reluctance from her initial reactions.

Given these problems, it is little wonder that Andy was not successful in working out win-win exchanges.

Though this analysis might seem a bit harsh on Andy, the task is not to allocate responsibility on one or the other of them. Initiative remains with junior partners, and in spite of the obstacles that Andy faced, he could have significantly increased the probability of building a more effective relationship—even some semblance of a partnership.

One way that Andy failed to embrace a partnership mind-set was by defining his role as performing in his area only. He didn't think that it was his responsibility to integrate Gwen in this job or to turn her into a better manager. Instead, his goal was only to find ways to get her to do what he wanted. He complained that Gwen wasn't like Cathy—the perfect boss for him.

Second, Andy didn't try to understand the pressures Gwen might have been under. This was a new job probably requiring different competencies than she had developed as a controller (and in a different country). That alone would be challenging, but to follow a great leader like Cathy could be daunting. It appears that Andy did nothing but negatively judge her—which did nothing to make her feel confident about how she was doing.

What could Andy have done differently? One would have to be somewhat insensitive not to recognize that Gwen probably felt highly vulnerable in her new position. He wouldn't overtly have to say that— that might be too "touchy-feely" for somebody who lived by the "stiff upper lip" rule—but he could have realized her concern—and then shown it. He might have then seen her "micromanaging" not as compulsive, but as a result of feeling pressure to perform.

It also would have helped Andy to understand that numbers and facts were a key currency for Gwen. They made her feel surer of herself and were probably why she talked to his direct reports. When a boss wants data, you don't want to withhold it out of a need for autonomy; rather, you should flood the boss as a way to trade for more freedom.

And why was the fact that Andy was excluded from meetings Gwen's fault in his eyes? People change when it is in their best interest; did he talk to Gwen about how keeping him out might prevent her from gaining what she wanted? A partner orientation forces you to move beyond "what is best for me" to "what is best for us."

Andy also could have been aware of Gwen's problem-solving style, which appears to be silently collecting information, and not sharing her concerns. One approach would be to initiate preliminary meetings where he explicitly asks what concerns she has and what information she needs. Partners take the responsibility of working out alternative approaches rather than expecting the boss always to do things "right."

Once Gwen knows that Andy is on her side, she might be willing to open up a bit. This would be especially likely if he could legitimize that discussion about gathering information by showing understanding. "It must have been tough taking on this assignment." If Gwen were willing to specify her concerns, they could establish a more collegial relationship. The lack of personal connection won't be so tough to swallow once Andy understands that the lack probably has nothing to do with him or with Gwen's personality. Understanding the boss's context unhooks you from making personal attributions too readily.

But What If I Have a Truly Toxic Boss?

Sometimes nothing works. There are some truly impossible bosses who cannot admit their own deficiencies, so mean that they do not care about the learning or satisfaction of their direct reports, so insecure that they try to take claim for what you do, or so incompetent that even if they are willing to be influenced, they are hopeless. If you are dealing with one of those, your best option may be to do what you have to in order to protect yourself as soon as possible. However, it's always a good idea to do everything you can to discern whether that person is genuinely rotten, or just someone whose behavior appears that way—and who you can move with the proper approach. Toxicity was the assumption that Mary Quinn (Chapter 1) made until she screwed up her courage and confronted her boss directly and found that they could build a workable (although not close) relationship. Similarly, Matt Larson (Chapter 4) viewed his boss as "Dr. Death," but ultimately discovered that he could work with and actually learn from her. This book has given you various options for discerning whether your boss is merely difficult or truly impossible. Whereas understanding their world can provide useful information, having open dialogue provides crucial firsthand evidence about whether a relationship is possible. It can be hard to engage in such a direct conversation; you don't want to jeopardize any relationships if you depend completely on this job.

You can lessen this dependency, however, when you have options. It's always wise to accumulate "walkaway money" so that you will not be afraid to act when you are stuck in a terrible situation. Do you have a strong network within the company where you could go for support or transfer—or any other kind of backup plan?

Keep in mind as well that bullies tend to bully when they know that they can get away with it. Knowing that your world will not end if this job does could actually provide the impetus you need to confront that individual. This was the situation that upper-middle manager Ned faced. He was hired by a major construction company to develop their market and was sent to Atlanta to grow their southeast area. As it turned out, the major challenge was not with the market, but with Bill, southeast regional director and Ned's boss:

> Bill doesn't listen to our input, changes our decisions, and even gives orders to our direct reports. He flies down regularly from DC and gets deep into the details, but makes decisions without really knowing what we have planned. It takes days to straighten out the messes he causes.
>
> When we raise our concerns, Bill goes ballistic and yells. He sees himself as the major dealmaker, when *we* are actually closer to the customer and see the opportunities. He thinks that he knows more than we do, and interferes with negotiations.
>
> I am not sure what to do. I could leave; it wouldn't be that hard for me to find another job. But I want to see if I can work this out.

Ned first collected some data. He made some informal inquiries with the internal contacts that he had made and discovered that Bill had a mixed performance record in this company. He had already alienated two of the other regional directors, who said that they would never work with him again. He was a good solo deal-maker, but he hadn't been so successful in developing other areas.

Ned knew that he could develop the greater Atlanta region if Bill would only stop interfering. They were aligned around the same goals, even though they differed on means—which meant that the potential for partnership did exist. Furthermore, Ned was good at building horizontal (and diagonal) relationships, so perhaps he would be better at reaching out to other regions than Bill could. This analysis indicated that Bill needed Ned as much (if not more) than Ned needed Bill. Ned decided to send Bill the following memo:

> Bill,
>
> I want to follow up on our conversation from last week. I will schedule a few hours for us to have uninterrupted conversation during your visit next week. As you can probably tell, I am neither comfortable nor satisfied with how we are working together. I am sure that there are things that frustrate you about me, and I want to know what they are. We must explore this so that we can avoid counterproductive actions and results, and instead work to build momentum toward having a successful and collaborative operation. I will cite specific examples, because I know these are more helpful to you. While I hope that this e-mail doesn't feel too solemn, I do hope it clearly conveys its serious nature. Thank you, ahead of time.
>
> —Ned

The meeting was difficult and did not produce the turnaround that Ned had hoped. However, he was pleased with how he responded.

> In hindsight, I am happy with how I was able to be direct, honest, and dispassionate. We kept it professional and focused on his behavior's negative impact. Moreover, I took the feedback I asked for and received from Bill without becoming defensive. I let him know that I agreed with his assessment and wanted to work on it more. (He seemed to be a bit taken aback by my reactions.)
>
> Bill responded defensively, denied that problems existed, or said that he was not inclined to change. Over the course of the two hours, I actually felt more and more comfortable as his actions provided perfect examples of his traits which are so counterproductive. The conversation confirmed that I simply do not think he has the ability, nor desire, to operate the division and establish a productive culture. I left with an odd feeling that I'm comfortable with the notion of leaving the company.
>
> But before I do, I think it is my responsibility to take my concerns to his boss, the CEO. I do not know where that would

lead, but I would be negligent in my role's duties if I didn't raise the red flag.

Ned then sent an e-mail to Mark, the company president, laying out his concerns about "the company's ability to find success in the Southeast." He said that he had discussed this with Bill, but felt that it went nowhere and was now asking for a face-to-face meeting with Mark.

I write to ask for time to confidentially speak with you. I need to convey the concerns I have regarding Bill as they have significant implications on our company's ability to find success in the Southeast. I have brought my concerns to Bill's attention numerous times. In doing so, I have worked to be direct, honest, and dispassionate; however, I have only seen defensiveness, inability to acknowledge the problems, and continued counterproductive behavior. After 5-plus months of this, I am disappointed to have no option left but to elevate this to your attention.

I suspect that Bill will not react well to my contacting you. As a result, I would suggest we have our discussion prior to your outreach to him. I do think it would be helpful for you to hear the impressions of others within this division, as I believe my concerns are shared and the problems are widespread.

I am willing to take a day off and fly myself up to New York to visit, as I suspect this may be best explored in person. I look forward to hearing from you.

—Ned

Five hours later, Ned's phone rang; it was the CEO. "We had a 25-minute conversation where he asked me a series of concerned questions. I suggested that he also check with other managers so he didn't have to rely only on my word. We agreed that I would fly up on Monday."

The Monday meeting lasted more than an hour. I laid out all the issues and concluded by saying that I didn't think we could scale our business in the way we all wanted. I actually said that I would not approve the pending business plan because I didn't think we would be able to efficiently mitigate risk to warrant the seven-figure investment he would be making into *my* new territory. That honesty and willingness to speak against my own short-term interests seem to really have struck him.

Mark did a great job of listening, and asking questions that I felt were genuine and valid. When I went home, I e-mailed Bill: "In the interest of being totally transparent, I want to tell you that I met with the CEO and laid out my concerns."

I don't know what will happen—what Bill will do and what Mark will do—but I feel good about what I did. It was clean and aboveboard. I also think any of the outcomes will be good. Even if Bill fires me, I did my best and can get another job.

As we go to press, we still don't know the eventual outcome, but Ned says he can live with any of the outcomes. He might have gotten through to Bill to make him more receptive to looking at his leadership style. Mark might transfer Bill, or Ned might leave. Ned concluded, "I can leave with my head high knowing that I did what I thought was best for the company and for the people in my department."

Your Fallback Position

Sometimes, of course, you can't take the steps that Ned did. Your only option might be to stick it out until your toxic boss leaves or external conditions change. However, there are still ways to protect yourself:

- **Give your manager what he or she wants.** Even though your desire to cooperate is at an all-time low, you're more likely to survive if you do what your boss wants. Frame all conversations in terms of how what you are doing, not doing, or want to do will help the boss.

- **Document.** If you have a boss who "forgets" agreements or rewrites history, you should document agreements after a meeting. A follow-up e-mail saying, "I think this is what we agreed to" can clear up immediate confusion and be a useful reference on future disagreements.

- **Be careful about being vulnerable.** We have seen a few narcissistic but charismatic leaders who can turn it on and quite seductively charm disaffected subordinates—until the next time they revert back to their own self-centered behavior. Being seduced into openness and then getting slapped down causes a great deal of pain. You must always be on guard.

- **Establish maximum distance from your boss.** Another possibility is to work hard to find ways to get assigned to an area or project that requires little interaction with the boss. Negotiate the desired end product in terms of specific measurable objectives and a reporting timetable. Working this out ahead of time both protects you and decreases interactions.

- **Depersonalize.** Keep reminding yourself that in this case, it isn't about you; a truly toxic person spreads poison indiscriminately, and in the long run, ends up swallowing it too. Be patient.

- **Compensate or offset.** Find a way to compensate for specific things that drive you crazy. Anticipate and work around, preemptively doing what is needed to create sufficient space.

None of this is pleasant, but remember—the only certainties in life are death and taxes. As bad as a situation may be, "this too shall pass."

In the next section of the book, we extend the basic ideas about dealing with powerful people to influencing those more distant and inaccessible than your boss, such as senior executives in or out of your organization.

Influencing Powerful People

CHAPTER

10

Framing Your Change Strategy

Fitting Your Approach to the Players

This chapter covers the ways you can deal with more distant powerful people. Because these individuals are less obligated to you, and not entirely sure of what you can do for them, this can be more of a challenge than working with your own boss.

If your goal is to change your organization for the better, you're going to need help making these changes—specifically, from people who matter. You need to determine which individuals can either help or hinder you, who to take on, and in what order. This chapter will explore what matters to these people, and how you can use this information to get them on board.

Let's look at the problem facing Kelly Prescott, senior regional account manager at a large international pharmaceutical company. Kelly was trying to win approval for a deal with a very tough customer, but not getting far with her boss's boss, the senior director of national accounts. She thought he was being a jerk.

> Before I can develop a contract with customers, I need to get my manager Amy's buy-in. We then participate in conference calls or meetings to gain final approval. I then go back and forth with my customers before we finally strike a deal.
>
> Recently, I was going through a very tough business case with Amy's boss, the senior director of national accounts, and he was not budging. He didn't seem to want to finalize the contract proposal for my customer. I knew my customers were going to be really upset; we were putting them in a situation where they essentially had no other option. I thought my boss's boss was impossible, unsupportive, and providing totally unrealistic expectations.
>
> After reflecting a bit, however, I realized that I needed to step in his shoes for a moment. His task as head of our department is our financial bottom line. We were in a dire fiscal situation at my company; it was a matter of survival. He was looking out for the company's best interests.
>
> Though it wasn't normal protocol, I got my manager's approval to approach her boss at our face-to-face meeting. I needed to prepare, have room to concede, and anchor hard in the beginning. Most importantly, I needed to keep my emotion out of it. In the end, he was so impressed that I approached him, had done my homework, had been prepared, and sold so hard, that he gave in on a couple of the points.
>
> I learned through this situation that upper management's motives might not always be what I want to hear. It's their job to be tough, inflexible, and even a bit unrealistic at times. I also realize now how important it is to practice beforehand and remain unemotional.

Kelly had earned the trust of the first stakeholder—her boss— and then had to work on her boss's boss. She realized while preparing that the latter was heavily influenced by senior management and the company's current state. She was then able to depersonalize the issue and to work out an approach that he would take seriously.

One of the first steps in the influence process is to determine who the relevant stakeholders are. This isn't that difficult when it is your boss; however, it can take close examination as you deal with senior managers, in or outside your organization. The more thoroughly you do your homework on this, the more prepared you will be. There are likely to be many stakeholders, each with his or her own particular concerns. You need to develop plans for identifying who they are, what they want, who to approach first, and how you will approach them. If you fail to identify powerful stakeholders from the beginning, you're apt to be unpleasantly surprised.

This can happen to very capable people. For example, "Marie Truffaut" is a smart, intense manager in a very large diversified investment firm. Some of the firm's investments are in deals put together by other big players. She was recently

> . . . tasked with looking at the next fundraiser with a manager with whom we've worked for six years. I don't see them as a good investor; they are at the bottom third of their peers, have lots of ego, spin, and are hard to deal with.
>
> We discussed what we had to believe in order to invest in this fund, and knew it would be tough. While one of our larger older deals was with them, and it brought in 3.5 times our investment, the other six with them hadn't done so well. Our new deal team did their research and decided not to invest.

Marie had been so focused on evaluating the merits of the new deal being offered (and so irritated by the past arrogant behavior of the fund manager) that she hadn't thought about *her own* senior management. To her surprise, they were hard to convince that her firm should not go ahead.

> I hadn't realized that our own organization might not want to hear a *no*. Their reaction was: "How can we say *no* now after all the

deals we have done with them? Investing with him might strike it big again, and he is well connected for other possible deals." The fund manager is the kind of person likely to go right over my head to the top of our organization if we say no or make the terms as tough as I think we should. I didn't sufficiently anticipate senior people's thinking to see the challenge going forward.[1]

Marie was forced to figure out how to influence the internal senior managers as well as the fund manager. She might have gone about the evaluation of the deal differently had she figured out from the beginning who would care about the decision.

Failing to Identify Key Stakeholders— in or outside of the Company—Can Be Extremely Costly

Take the case of "HemoSeptrix," a biotechnology company based in the Cleveland area, whose failure to understand its own peripheral environment was profoundly damaging to its fortunes. [*Disclaimer: The names of this company and the people involved, as well as specific facts of the case, have been changed for privacy reasons; nonetheless, the details concerning the events that unfolded are true as provided by a person close to the situation. The story is presented as a cautionary tale for those thinking about possible impacts of stakeholders.*]

HemoSeptrix was created in 2001 to use the mapping of the human genome to develop a cure for a deadly blood disease that had no good treatment option. As with all such companies, everything is pointed toward eventually getting Food and Drug Administration (FDA) approval for the drug, once the company has developed a prototype, and passed through Phase 1, 2, and 3 testing. The entire process often takes 10 to 15 years or longer.

The company had been founded by Dr. Desmond Baker, a brilliant but extraordinarily difficult and irascible researcher in hematology, and Dr. Walter Beckman, a former professor and prominent venture capitalist. Baker's discoveries at Case Western University showed promise of being able to stop the course of sepsis in postsurgical patients, and if it worked and was approved by the FDA, would become a blockbuster product surpassing $1 billion per year in sales.

Difficult Founder

Although acclaimed as a brilliant researcher, Dr. Baker was widely disliked within the hematology community. Seen by his peers as arrogant, distant, and aloof, and by his students as explosive and dictatorial in the lab, he had few friends among his colleagues. He seldom attended scholarly congresses (unless as an invited speaker), and was feared for his famous "acid pen" as a journal peer reviewer. Many promising scientists had felt the sting of his editorials and letters in those journals as well, sometimes to their lasting professional detriment. Two such scientists, Dr. Ram Chandran and Dr. Bronwyn Chambers, later became close collaborators and key opinion leaders (KOLs) in the field in their own right, despite their difficult early encounters with Baker. (Key opinion leaders are physicians who influence their peers' medical practice.)

Although not without complications, the Phase 1 and 2 results were promising, but the Phase 3 trials started more slowly than anticipated. Getting hemataceptin to patients during the critical phases of sepsis proved logistically challenging, and (as with previous trials in sepsis) the wide variety of patients with the condition sometimes made it difficult to determine which patients fell within the trial's scope. The HemoSeptrix team spent many sleepless nights seeking ways to get the trials back on track.

As the trials fell behind and pressure on the company mounted, Baker's behavior changed dramatically. He became even more impatient than usual, and increasingly unpleasant to staffers, the board, investors, and even to Beckham. After receiving his third call in one week from board members complaining about Baker's insults, Beckham admonished Baker, "Start behaving yourself. You're alienating everyone in your path with your insults and tantrums—including some very canny people who have invested faith, time, and money in you and HemoSeptrix, and who deserve your respect. And it has to stop. Now."

Baker lashed out. "How *dare* you? I'm the *only* engine this company has. I'm the *only* reason we're already in Phase 3, and I'm the *only* one who can drive this home. I've worked 18-hour days for years to move this compound forward, and now you're threatening me because I don't suffer fools and let them know it? This conversation is beneath you, Walt," he said angrily. Beckham sighed. "Dez, I've been in this business for a long time, and if I've learned anything, it's not to anger people unnecessarily. You'll never know *when* it'll come back to bite you, but I can assure you—it *always* will."

Two weeks later a young researcher published a review article in a second-tier journal that critiqued the methodology for data analysis used by Dr. Baker and his students (including HemoSeptrix lead biometrician, Dr. Sho Mineta) in the last article Baker wrote while still at Case Western. Baker dashed off a scathing letter to the journal, savagely chastising the young researcher for her "temerity" and "superficial, flawed, and sophomoric thinking." Two weeks after that, he ridiculed her from the podium at the annual meeting of the American Hematological Association (AHA), where he had been invited to speak on hemataceptin. The young scientist considered suing Baker for defamation but, fearing further retaliation, deferred.

In the audience at the AHA meeting that day was Peter Chen, an eminent biostatistician often called upon by the FDA to assess the validity of statistical models and conclusions submitted by drug companies. Angered by what he considered Baker's bullying, Chen evaluated the data in question and, although unable to confirm all the woman's arguments, he too found flaws that raised fundamental questions about Baker's conclusions.

Although Chen did not publish his findings, he did include several slides in a lecture shortly thereafter to doctoral candidates. The slides, captioned "How Many in Baker's Dozen? We May Never Know," mentioned Baker and Sho Mineta by name, and subtly implied that some of the data might have been intentionally misrepresented to strengthen the writers' conclusions. The slides were circulated widely on the Internet and resulted in a number of thoughtful, and some outraged, letters and e-mails within the academic hematology community. Among the writers were Dr. Chandran and Dr. Chambers, who felt some vindication for Baker's past treatment of them. Completely absorbed with the Phase 3 delays, Baker ignored Chen's slides and the controversy that followed.

Beckham, however, did not ignore it. He assembled the board and gave Baker an ultimatum—quit or be fired. "Bullying a young woman on a national stage is so unbecoming a CEO, I can scarcely believe you did it. The damage you've done to HemoSeptrix is substantial. I'm sorry, Dez, but you have to go." After some negotiation, they agreed that Baker would continue to be a "consultant" to HemoSeptrix. They agreed as well that he would retain a substantial equity stake in the company and a royalty stream from the commercialization of hemataceptin.

Progress after Baker

With Baker gone, they hired Jonathon Schwartzman, a new, nonscientific, professional CEO to continue the work. After overcoming many challenges, HemoSeptrix made it through Phase 3 trials after four more years, with good but not great or unambiguous results. The 10,000-page application went to the preliminary advisory committee of the FDA, which wrestled with it (at least in part because of the controversies about the data analysis), but finally sent it to the FDA with a positive recommendation. This kind of recommendation resulted in FDA approval 85 percent of the time. Everyone at the company was jubilant and excited both about being able to bring a lifesaving drug to market and the potential financial payoff for their long hours of work.

Known Stakeholders Ignored—At Great Cost

Part of the FDA process was seeking the opinions of the experts in the field (KOLs). After the advisory committee recommendation, two of the leading experts, Drs. Chandran and Chambers, who had fought with and thoroughly disliked Dr. Baker, the founder, wrote very strong negative letters to the chair of the FDA about not trusting the reported results. They also worked on the related scientific community to raise doubts about the integrity of the company and the data, even though Dr. Baker was no longer part of it. The result of these letters and the surrounding controversy led the FDA, on the basis of inconsistent results in two trials, to require an additional confirmatory Phase 3 study before reconsidering hemataceptin for approval. The setback would cost the company years, tens of millions of dollars, and any hope of a prompt acquisition.

Many in the company knew that outside experts would be listened to, yet they ignored who the relevant stakeholders in the field were and what their possible responses might be. If they had considered this, the leaders within the company could have talked to them, brought them data, reassured them about the distancing of the founder, and done a variety of things to ensure that they would at least get a fair and objective hearing. Their failure to identify and address concerns of the important stakeholders has led to the need to redo and extend Phase 3 testing, at a cost of many millions of dollars.

In the words of a senior company executive, in rueful hindsight, could all this have been avoided?

> Simply put: *Yes*. Had the HemoSeptrix team taken the time to look, they easily could have found those who would influence the FDA against them and either made those people allies or, at the very least, neutralized their power over the decision. And the clues were *everywhere*.

It's vital to keep your eye on the ball; however, it can sometimes cause you to miss some key players. External stakeholders and groups have the potential to affect any organization or critical change project. For example, when clothing company Victoria's Secret was attacked by the Forest Ethics Campaign for not using recycled paper in its catalogs, many of its executives wanted to ignore them, but when people started picketing in front of their stores, they realized this was not a good idea. Every company lives in an ecosystem that has multiple stakeholders who can be more or less visible and active—but who *must* be identified. Finding relevant stakeholders, in or out of the organization, is a critical task. And the reasoning and analytical process is the same whatever their level of power.

Start with a Power Map

You must start by figuring out what you want to accomplish and who is involved in that issue—people who need to cooperate in some way, those who should be informed or consulted, and those who will be directly impacted by what you're doing. See Tables 10.1 and 10.2. It is worth being overinclusive in the beginning, adding anyone who might be an important influencer of the person or people you want to directly influence. As you go further, you may be able to eliminate some of these people, and keep the task from becoming too overwhelming. But if you are taking on a large issue, the relevant list may be quite extensive.

Stakeholder Power

Conduct a preliminary assessment of each stakeholder's power. How much access to information, resources, and people do they have? What is your relative power in relation to each? (Keep in mind that you may

TABLE 10.1 Power Map

	Influence result required:	Need to influence is: (select one of next columns)	Helpful not necessary	Can work around	Ignore or wall off
Person 1					
Person 2					
. . . Person n					

well be able to increase this as you go along). Can you continue without their cooperation? Would their cooperation be helpful but not necessary to have? Or can you work around that stakeholder?

Partnership Mind-Set

Don't forget that you need to approach even those who appear to be significant active blockers with a partnership mind-set. When people are resisting, it can be hard to sustain real concern for them and their interests. They might have a piece of knowledge or perspective that could make your proposal even stronger and more likely to be accepted by the "powers that be." Don't treat them as enemies until you can be sure that they have no potential organizational benefit.

You need to carefully examine the interests, power, knowledge, and agendas of every relevant individual, group, or organizational stakeholder—and determine who influences others. Although you might not be able to sway a powerful person, he or she might respond to someone else's argument. Who has those connections? This complete analysis is critical for selling ideas or proposals, gaining backing for projects, neutralizing resistance, or otherwise making a difference.

Determining exactly what matters to the stakeholders can be an intensive process. (We will show more about how to do this in the next chapter, "What Do the Powerful Care About?") Though it was extraordinarily complicated for Kelly Prescott, it required that she check with colleagues to get a sense of what mattered to her boss's boss. She was able to do this once she considered what his role made him value.

TABLE 10.2   Power Map (Part 2)

	Power	Interests/ Agendas	Knowledge	Connections
Person 1				
Person 2				
Person n				

The following are some questions that will help determine stakeholder interests:

- What is the issue or set of issues at stake?
- Who are the relevant stakeholders?
- What are their interests/stakes?
- What is the intensity with which the stake is held?
- What claims come with the stake?
- What differences and similarities exist across these stakes/stakeholders? (This is helpful if they are all going to be dipping their oar into the issue.)
- How can these stakeholders affect the issue?
- What actions can you or your organization take to affect the interests of each relevant stakeholder?
- What are your fallback plans?[2]

There are some other things you can do to collect data on needs in the organization when they are not immediately apparent. As we have already suggested in previous chapters, the wider the net of relationships you can build before you need them, the easier it will be to figure out what people care about and make exchanges with them. But if you do not already have these relationships, you can always do some research. Ask people you *do* know what the various stakeholders pay attention to, how they like to be approached, and what land mines to avoid. Asking people for this kind of information usually deepens previous relationships. It is a form of giving currency to ask for information because it assumes the person you are asking is important or astute enough to know the answer.

This process should allow you to identify people who can help you target the right individuals. Just be sure to be careful about how you ask and explain your interest in these people. If you frame it in terms of benefits to the organization rather than a personal power grab, word may get to your influence targets and dispose them favorably to your approach.

Of course, you need to be just a bit cautious about the quality of the information you are receiving, and beware of rumors or loose opinions that could lead you in the wrong direction. For example, "Monica Ashley," an employee in charge of a radical product development effort at "Heal-Inc.," was opposed by a powerful senior scientist who her boss and others said was impossible to influence. As a result, she never really talked to this man—and her failure to at least try to partially neutralize him increased his opposition and made her life quite miserable.[3] The moral here—make sure you can trust the accuracy of your sources, or at least take them with a grain of salt, and decide whether to augment information with some direct data collection.

Sequencing of Action

The map you've developed can help you develop a strategy. Who will you start with? Are there any in the critical path who need to be influenced before you can go forward with any hope of succeeding? Are there any stakeholders you can ignore, or only need to neutralize? Do you have access to the critical ones? If not, how can you gain it?

It will help the process if you determine in which of the following categories your stakeholders fit:

- **Innovators** (likely to be favoring change and out front in trying ideas)
- **Early adopters** (ready to test new ideas)
- **Early majority** (open-minded and will go with what looks promising)
- **Late majority** (get on board once they see things moving in a new direction)
- **Resistors** (hold out against what they don't like or don't see how to use)[4]

You can use this scheme to determine where you stand, and who requires what kind of influence attention. Once the early majority is on board, the change crosses a tipping point that makes it likely to be adopted. This can help you sequence those you have to influence; you need innovators and early adopters on board to get some momentum started, so it helps to identify their interests early and make sure they are supportive. You can pay less attention early to likely blockers, but be sure to not make them feel excluded lest they dig in for reasons that have little to do with your actual concept.

The following scenario provides an example of how to consider stakeholders and their needs. Jo Ann Herold was chief marketing officer at the HoneyBaked Ham Company, where she sold marketing plans internally.

Because Herold needed a lot of people to cooperate, she concentrated on doing what was needed to move varying constituents:

> I have learned to adapt presentations to the people in the room. Everyone is there with a different hat and talking from their perspective. I try to think about how it will affect each person, and find a way to articulate how it will impact their area. How can I address their issues up front?
>
> Take, for example, the catalog. Our sales were not hitting where we wanted last year, so we introduced a shipping incentive at the last minute. We knew that it would hurt our bottom line if it didn't get results. I worked with our finance department to determine the incentive's financial impact. I worked with operations to be sure they were ready to pack the extra boxes, and with ops folks to be sure they were staffed for extra sales. I worked with purchasing to make sure the suppliers had the right inventory. I had to work with the marketing team to get the e-mail blast out, and made sure the phones were staffed so we could take extra orders. I was able to influence a lot of people to make it happen quickly.
>
> You need to speak others' language. I know that I have to understand how the functions fit in the bigger picture; the more I know, the more effective I am. Without that understanding, marketing people are labeled as "wacky." You can be very effective

when you understand the totality of the business—and realize that internal customers are as important as external.[5]

This kind of thought process often sounds obvious after the fact, but it can be hard to maintain when you are passionate about how wonderful your idea or plan or project is. It can feel frustrating to slow down enough to persuade powerful senior people who may be driven by different goals, perspectives, vision, preoccupations, and a number of factors that are not automatically visible to you. That's why it's so essential to identify all possible stakeholders and their concerns.

The following is a positive example of working out the complexities for a tough cross-divisional assignment with lessons in influence from a sophisticated manager named "Lucia Emerson." She works at "Grandetech," a very large international high-tech manufacturing organization. Her usual job is in supply chain in a program management role, always leading virtual teams, with sites all over the globe.

Influence across Three Divisions

My task was to fix the existing SAP-based solution for managing outside contractors. We use up to 50,000 contract employees at once, and the process was so complex that one warehouse couldn't even open because none of the contractors' badges worked and people couldn't get into the facility.

Three key decision makers owned everything: *Information Technology* (IT)—sustaining technical support; *Materials*—manages all transactions related to headcount; and the biggest group, *Corporate Services*—all facilities management (half of Grandetech contractors: janitorial, facilities, etc.). They were spending more time on managing the system because of the volumes, and were the loudest stakeholders.

Getting all three on the same page was one of the toughest challenges I have faced. IT wanted it fastest and cheapest in terms of development resources to design, launch, and maintain it. The existing tool was so disastrous that they were getting four times as many calls to the help line as they would with similar tools, and had to hire more help just to answer calls. My research showed that the best idea would need more resources in the beginning, but ought to be much less expensive to maintain. I approached IT with the following tactic: if you will just let us spend more upfront, we can get a solution that can minimize the ongoing resources needed.

The biggest stake for my group, Materials, was risking control; they had to see that the operating units stayed within contractual terms, because the contract workers are at our sites or on our network. They needed to see us mitigating risk appropriately while running the business smoothly. The problem was that the existing tool dealt too heavily with risk—at the expense of holding up our business.

The primary driver for Corporate Services was running our facilities and answering questions from the field, such as: How will I keep my construction project on schedule, get new fab open, not disrupt my cafeteria, etc.? Risk is not as pressing for this group. They wanted people in the door easily and quickly, with the least time to manage. So we had to come up with one solution that took these three totally different perspectives into account.

This was a difficult assignment, and here's how I went about it:

We analyzed several alternative solutions, and performed a usability study on the existing system. We recorded audio of actually bringing a contract person in the door and asking the employee to think out loud as they were doing it, while measuring keystrokes. It was a really effective tool for capturing the

(continued)

(*continued*)

reality of the current system; the challenge for us was to do it in a convincing way.

To make the trade-offs, the team agreed on high-level decision criteria, using a tool called the cause-effect template. We got one set of scores for each option and weighted them, which gave us a numerical value and a way to quantify qualitative criteria. It also provided a way to talk; the divisions can't disagree if they have been part of the process all the way, even when they don't necessarily like the conclusion. The build option came out 30 percent better.

We also shot user videos. Letting executives see relatively senior managers talking out loud, saying "I don't know where to go next," was very effective in getting even IT to accept that we couldn't just fix the SAP system, so spending was needed. It helped Materials understand that risk mitigation had to happen *along with* efficiency and usability.

I recommended scrapping SAP and going with an internally custom-built solution, using what we learned from SAP, but *balancing* risk and usability. They eventually settled with my approach, and built a system from the ground up as a custom app.

I hadn't realized at the beginning just how challenging a situation I was facing. But it put me on the map through the VP level; I like hard work, when there is ambiguity and difficulty to get agreement. I am getting more benefits from the increase in reputation as we go. The Corporate Services VP and I have crossed paths several times now, just because of that. For example, he saw me at a meeting a while back, and said, "Oh great, Lucia is here, we will be fine." Reputation makes a difference. I look at every influence situation as an opportunity to build credibility. It is definitely not just about having a fancy technique; our culture has integrity at the heart, so you have to do the work, have your data, and can't fake it.

Remember, good work has to be paired with all the stakeholder planning and influencing activities.

We turn next to a more detailed view of how to figure out just what is important to each of the powerful people you need to influence. This is an extension of the basic approach spelled out in our influence model in Chapter 4, but even more focused on distant high-powered people who you may have to diagnose from a distance.

CHAPTER

11

What Do the Powerful Care About?

The bigger the power gap between you and the other person, the less likely it is that you will be able to influence him or her. You need to figure out what you have to offer. If you aren't in a position to know much about what the other party values, you won't know how to appeal to what matters to that person. When trying to see what shapes the powerful person's currencies, your best bet is to try to understand his or her context—even though that world may seem distant and unfamiliar to yours.

This chapter provides some analytic questions to ask to try to determine their world, as well as some generic information about the types of things that relatively powerful people—especially those near the top of their organizations—think about. Of course, you want to test out your assumptions before you act upon them and then fit them to the individual. But you might only get a brief moment with this person, so the better you connect with him or her—the better your odds for success will be.

Sometimes you can do homework beforehand—whether this includes researching on your own or finding information through other people. But it isn't always possible to be so informed in advance. And if you don't frame a situation as these people see it, it's often impossible to engage in further conversation. That's what makes it so hard to influence relatively powerful people; they know what they value, and do not want to deal with anyone who isn't working from a similar set of assumptions and values. Even if you are doing good work on your level, you must be fully aware of what is on the mind of the person above. Not only do you want to understand that person's world; you must also make sure that you are not acting on something that seemed like a good idea solely from *your* perspective, and missing wider or different objectives. Where you sit shapes where you stand; try to anticipate how it looks from above.

There are several contextual factors that you can use to try to do diagnosis from a distance, all of which are an extension of the influence model introduced in Chapter 4. However, they're applied here to senior people who are even more likely to reflect pressures from external forces—the competition's actions, industry trends, and so on. You should be able to find a good amount of this information in internal documents or via colleagues if the senior person is in your own organization. You may have to work harder at gathering information for someone outside; however, asking around can help you find the answers. One tactic is to see if the person's gatekeeper is willing to talk with you. If you are friendly enough and explain why you're interested, the gatekeeper might just be amenable.

Always keep the following in mind: *in general, people most easily partner with people who they feel are like them.* One starting point to figure out what you have in common is to know what top managers generally value. Despite some variations, a good number of senior managers face similar issues and have similar interests and priorities, including the following:

- **A balance of the organization's costs, growth/innovation, and the building of future capacities.** This is a major task for senior managers. Overemphasis on any one of these competing areas will eventually harm the organization, although they have differing levels of importance at different times.

- **Major economic forces such as inflation, deflation, interest rates, and demand.** This is less of a concern during good times. However, external economic conditions can have a critical current or future impact on the organization.

- **Innovation, products and processes.** Finding, developing, and growing the products of the future, or inventing and implementing the processes to run the organization is an ongoing challenge. Many organizations are transitioning from selling stand-alone products to developing and selling complete solutions.

- **Overseas competition.** Increasing numbers of companies are discovering increasing direct competition and/or competition enabled by competitors' use of overseas companies, for materials, subassemblies, low-cost, or otherwise unavailable talent.

- **Outsourcing for costs, lowering of capital costs, and search for new markets.** It has become possible to outsource many more aspects of what organizations do; this issue raises a host of questions about costs, transportation time, reliability, and accuracy of communications—and some work is being brought back to the home country.

- **Talent acquisition and retention (workforce demographics issues: aging, skills, women, immigrants, and language).** Even in times of high unemployment, some industries are suffering from shortages of skilled individuals.

- **Sources of supply (oil, rare earths, metals, others).** Sudden shortages or wild price fluctuations can have a major impact.

- **Integrity and ethics, company reputation.** Companies that have ignored ethical and legal issues can wind up with great losses or scandal, with the behavior of top executives themselves under greater scrutiny.

- **Their own relationship to the board, those who finance the organization, the press, industry peers.** Top managers also are responsible to a variety of constituents who might have conflicting goals and strong ideas about judging company performance. If publicly owned, shareholders and the financial industry can be demanding critics, and share price can be a preoccupation. Private or family ownership has its own demands. And fears about what the press might focus on can also be a big worry.

- **Regulations, Sarbanes-Oxley Act, and health care and other government policies.** Even though clear regulations can make the life of top managers easier, they tend not to like feeling restricted, and the obligations and transparency forced by Sarbanes-Oxley and other government requirements can be very uncomfortable.

Although not a totally comprehensive list, these are the kinds of issues that generally concern senior executives. And because they will surely color what is on the minds of top management, they shape the criteria managers use to judge you. Your awareness of these and company-specific issues will make it more likely that top people will see you as a potential junior partner—one who is aware of the bigger picture.

These kinds of issues also tend to frame the way top managers think about the consequences of their actions. If the financial press is closely watching and judging every penny spent, then loosely promised benefits are not likely to be terribly convincing. On the other hand, it may appear too shortsighted to offer precise, short-term benefits to a group trying to implement a new strategy. This is why you must link your proposal to current strategic efforts or preoccupations.

In short, think about what the audience cares about, and not just about the virtues of your product or idea as you see them.

You'll also want to know specifically the issues that matter to the particular individual or group you're targeting. What kinds of public statements do they make? What do the business press and financial analysts say about them? What is the proclaimed company strategy, vision, and values aspired to? What are the dominant senior managers' educational and work backgrounds? Based on their records, do you expect them to think about technology, sales potential, costs, brand, or something else first? Will they care more about the risks to implementing your proposal, or the potential gains? Will they care at all whether there is learning involved—or do only results matter?

The following section lists some other areas to investigate that can lead to good guesstimates of what matters to these important people.

Factors in the Organizational World That Shape the Currencies of Powerful People

- Their actual job. What are the specific tasks they are expected to perform (or choose to do)?
  - Do they spend a high percentage of their time in the public eye?
  - Or are they mainly internally focused?
  - Do they spend time talking with and listening to organization members' concerns? If this person prefers to seem "approachable," he or she will probably want you to use a friendlier style.
- What do the company and industry cultures emphasize?
  - What is considered appropriate behavior? For example, how risk-taking and innovative are people expected to be? Is it essential to follow hierarchy and protocol?
  - Don't stereotype too readily, though; some companies run counter to their industries and value quite different things from their industry practices. Know the specifics of your target.
- What are the powerful party's work surroundings?
  - Does the person work in a closely guarded area with several layers of people to go through in order to gain access, or work in an open area and frequently mingle with employees?

- Are they using honed skills or does the position call for them to do things they have not done much before?
  - Have they worked in the same company/organization and industry for a long time or is this a move? Those who have been with a particular company or industry for a while tend to be more set in their ways than those who have experienced discontinuities in their careers.
- Is there a record of what the organization's board wanted when it selected the person for the job? What shortcomings of the previous incumbent were being countered?
  - When people are hired at a high level, there are usually public statements from the board or company about why they are enthusiastic about the person selected. Was the board looking for continuity with the past leader or a sharp break? Because incoming executives are always eager to make their mark, they're likely to value anything that can enhance the goals that the board had in mind.
- Are there public speeches, annual reports, blogs, op-ed columns, or other records of this person declaring what he or she values? (Google is your friend in this instance!)
  - Most powerful people have extensive public records that can reveal a lot of what they care about. (We will provide further information about this in the next chapter.)

Are You Seeking to Influence People inside or outside the Organization? About One Event, or Multiple Issues?

If you are trying to influence people within the organization about a single change effort, the most powerful currencies are likely to be around the business issues described above. You need to make the best business case—one that takes organizational context into account.

Though you are unlikely to immediately build a *personal* connection, if you can find commonalities or encounter one another doing good work, it might ease the way.

If you are dealing outside your organization, you need to create instant credibility and connection, and often, begin a longer-term, more complex relationship. You might be building a strategic alliance around specific outcomes with a competitor, or working with others in the same trade association. Or you might be creating a consulting engagement. Some kind of a personal relationship may be a requirement. Even something as simple as just making a sale requires credibility and connection.

Neither lower-power insiders nor outsiders should confuse potential connection with the need to do good work. But how the proposed work is perceived is related to the way benefits are framed, and to how the presenter is seen, so understand as much as you can about what the powerful are likely to be thinking. People usually connect and spend time with others who share their values and interests. Don't turn yourself into a chameleon and feign interests that you don't have—that deceptiveness is usually quite transparent. Instead, search for areas in which you naturally have common interests and build on those. The following are some ways to assess what, in addition to their immediate business concerns, may be of importance to people you are seeking to influence.

Tracking Their Habitats

- What associations does the person belong to? With whom does he or she socialize and talk? Remember the adage: "By the company they keep, you will know them."

- Is the person part of the Chamber of Commerce? A particular trade association? A board member of any charities—that might include other powerful board members? What charity events does the person attend? How about country club memberships? What activities does that reflect: golf, tennis, swimming, boating?

- What about other hobbies? It isn't news that many in business play golf, sometimes quite seriously; others ski, attend film or art festivals, and many charity parties, where attendees buy expensive tickets as part of a quid pro quo arrangement with friends who in turn buy tickets from them.

- How and where people live also helps shape their desires and values. Do they reside in posh suburban homes, or urban buildings? Fancy vacation homes in the "right" spots? Expensive resorts?

- Do their possessions—jewelry, autos, art, clothes, etc.—put them in powerful company?

- You may get a good idea of what matters to the person by checking out these formal and informal "memberships." And, of course, some very powerful people do not associate so much with others like them—which is equally revealing.

- These social forces can help determine what the powerful person cares about, and the currencies to which he or she is likely to be receptive. Although the things that they value may never overtly come up as a topic of discussion, knowing about them can help you converse more confidently. You can also establish your credibility by commenting on their power. For example, an ironic (and complimentary) question like, "How do you pull that off?" can show that you appreciate their strength and skill.

- Table 11.1 is a useful (albeit general) guide for making a quick determination about powerful people. It can potentially help you determine your approach after you have done the kind of diagnosis we are recommending, combined with some firsthand observation. The table represents a series of admittedly slightly stereotyped leader styles and how to respond to each. Keep in mind that these styles are merely hypothetical constructs for the purposes of illustration; they present a more "black and white" version of the shades of gray you'll encounter in real-world behavior.

TABLE 11.1 Powerful Leaders Commonly Encountered in Selling Strategy Consulting

Stereotype or "Dominant Gene"	Defing Characteristics	Vehicles to Connect As Peer
1. Cerebral thinker	Ponders; "See them think"; Requires evidence	Let them "See you Think"; Research, data; Tell the Story
2. Experience-based loyalist	Life work lessons dominate; No"I"s. Rarely manages up; Focus is down; Rarely takes credit	Bring another experience-based person; company focused discussion—not business personal
3. Political survivalist	"I" dominates; Asks for political alliance; Company secondary;	Listen; do not commit to politics; Distance
4. Intergalactic driver	High energy; Idea person; Some ideas good; Evidence of action/results; Great person to be around	Ideas of your own; think alongside and intersect when possible; "Equal" energy;
5. Tyrannical emotionalist	Needs domination; not logical; Can be demeaning	Direct presentation distance; Search for key to settle down; Typically need to exit
6. Analytical follower	Talks in numbers; Lives in his or her calculations; a supporter of the leader	Charts; graphs; research studies; analysis of their operation; numbers
7. Glass half-full socializer (think insurance industry)	Mixes business and pleasure; Always up; Always sees the good; No problems; Opportunity only	Put them in their comfort location; Like to get inside scoop.
8. Conservative historian	"I remember when"; This "needs a lot of input"; "I will get back to you"	Tell a historical story; Indirect presentation; See person last!

Source: Created by Michael May, Accenture, now Babson College. Used with permission.

Although fairly general, the table can help determine powerful people's likely preferred style, telling you a lot about how they may want to be presented to or how they would like to receive proposals.

Use a Powerful Proposal Style Whether Dealing Internally or Externally

Unfortunately, many lower-power people experience fear when they have to impress top management. This usually prompts them to either freeze up and omit vital information, or to overpresent so as to seem as knowledgeable as possible. Yet top managers tend to be very impatient. They want presenters to have done their homework, but they seldom want to hear all the details first. If your assumptions don't make sense to them, all the homework you did is irrelevant.

Consider what Phil Juliano, previously vice president of marketing at Novell, learned about presenting to top managers:

> When dealing with a company's CEO, you don't throw a proposed approach without first level setting—that is, reminding the CEO of how you got to the new positioning. You want them to have confidence that you have done your homework. They want to be sure that their organization is solid. Don't share every wart or imperfection; discuss what you learned, document your conclusions, and never hide the data. However, CEOs know there is not perfect science in this imperfect world—so ambiguity comes with the territory.[1]

Phil learned, as is often the case, that the technical material so important to *him* in insuring good work wasn't necessarily relevant to the top people. Therefore, proposals to senior managers almost always need to:

- Be concise.
- Start with the conclusions and implications.
- Include the major assumptions behind the proposal.

- This can be challenging for people who find the specifics intriguing, or want senior people to know how hard they have worked. But nothing creates as much credibility as two basic things:

  1. Having a good track record for delivering

  2. Making compelling proposals that immediately reveal their expected benefits

You must always frame proposals in terms of solving organizational problems that powerful people care about. Though this is Sales 101, many specialists and experts don't like to think of themselves as selling.

You'll be even more effective with a positive track record. The executive team often knows less about what is being proposed than you do, so fall back on their general trust of how well you have come through in the past. Of course this is a bit of a Catch-22, because to have a good track record you need to have been supported, and to be supported it helps to have a good track record. However, you can always start on smaller projects, deliver more than is expected, and establish a reputation as someone who values business payoffs more than self-promotion.

If you happen to support something in which you truly believe but don't yet have the internal credibility, try to find credible allies to join you ahead of time. Make sure they have a significant role, because they probably know a thing or two (given their track record)—and give them plenty of visibility. And whether or not you have general credibility or are borrowing it, find ways to link your claimed outcomes to current concerns, strategies, or ongoing efforts. Great ideas that don't seem to connect to what is on the minds of the powerful are too often missed or pushed aside.

We have warned about the danger of being too fearful and not making your strongest case. But it is also an important skill to know when to back off, do more homework, work harder to connect to top management concerns, propose an alternative like a small pilot or entrepreneurial spinoff, wait for new senior leadership—or even when to leave.

Yet however you gauge what powerful people value, none of it helps if you can't get to talk with the people whose cooperation you want. Figuring out how to gain access is the subject of the next chapter.

12

Action Steps for Gaining Access to Powerful People

It can be incredibly frustrating to have a great idea—but to lack the ability to meet the people who can make it a reality. There are so many layers in some large organizations that people don't even try; they either just sit on their ideas or take them elsewhere. Their own supervisor might be blocking them; and some genuinely new ideas can take time for senior people to accept. In those cases, access becomes even more important.

This chapter focuses on how to get to the powerful people you want to influence. As we have noted, one of the best ways to gain access is by already having an outstanding reputation—which you do by establishing a strong track record for accomplishing what you commit to, and delivering more than promised. It also helps to constantly consider what's good for the organization rather than just for yourself. But even the best reputation may not extend high enough in the organization to gain needed access. This requires that you either tap your existing network of relationships or build stronger ones with new, potentially helpful people. Of course, building a relationship where the person is willing to help you is another kind of influence challenge that requires determining what others value—and working together to meet both of your goals. There are no shortcuts.

Furthermore, you often have to work your way up the hierarchy if you are selling a complex organizational proposal. If you have performed well, you might already have access to people slightly below the top who can help you get to the ultimate decision maker(s). This still poses an influence challenge, because there's no guarantee that they will buy in.

It is also important to remember that the various people you may encounter in your search for influence may all have suggestions for modifying your pitch. As you gather reactions and advice, listen hard and refrain from resisting. You will have to decide when to bend and adapt to their suggestions and when you need to stick to your ideas—or possibly find a new project to work on.

The Bold, Direct Approach

There frequently is no way to make a direct approach—and even when there is, the odds for success probably are not good. Nevertheless, two instructive and possibly inspiring examples are worth offering, because in each case anyone looking from the outside would have said that there was virtually no chance. We would hate for you to overlook the possibilities.

The first example was in the extremely hierarchical Toyota Motors. Suppose you are Peter Dames (introduced in Chapter 1), working in the technology area at Toyota Motor Sales USA before that company, or any automaker, has figured out how to best use the possibilities of electronics and the Internet. The company is cautious and traditional, and quite rule-bound, but selling lots of vehicles, with sales continuously rising. If you are Peter Dames, you don't think such growth will continue in the e-commerce age but need to create a sense of urgency in the company. Who do you have to win over to get more happening? The answer is: many people all over the U.S. operation. Dames started with his boss, Barbara Cooper, the newly hired chief information officer (CIO), who he assumed, as a new employee, would be interested in doing something different to make her mark. She reported that

> On my first day here . . . Peter . . . pokes his head in and asks, "Do you have an open-door policy?" . . . But Cooper instantly identified Dames as an ally . . .

Cooper knew that they had to educate those in the business about the value of e-commerce; because of his direct approach, she trusted him and gave him considerable latitude: "He understands that the mission isn't to deny the executive body, or to go around it, but to bring it along."[1]

Dames and his small team decided they needed to create a space where people in the company could see possibilities for digitized interactions with vendors, dealers, and others in the widely dispersed company.

They created what they called a sneaker meeting, a place where people could drop in to use computers and see what was possible. Dames's team was deliberately nervy and countercultural: "Toyota was suits and ties; we said this is part of our deal, doing things differently." Knowing they would need support from the top, and feeling impatient, they completely ignored the company expectation of making proposals only to one's boss, who would take it to his boss if he liked it, and so on up the line. Dames directly called the president's office and talked with the assistant, who he knew. "I've got something he needs to see, so get him down here for an hour." The assistant told the boss it would be interesting.

> We had a lot of issues we wanted to bring to his attention . . . Usually, people are hesitant to go to senior executives without an answer or a fully thought-out plan. But it didn't stop us. Afterwards, the president urged us to talk to the rest of the top executives and take them through the same discussion, the same experience.

Once the e-commerce team could boast about conducting sneaker meetings with senior management of the U.S. operation, people at all levels of the company began clamoring for invitations. Slowly, as people saw the possibilities, they tested functions in their own domains, and eventually, the concept spread to other Toyota offices, even in Japan.

There were numerous reasons for Dames's courage to take the risk of going directly to the president. He knew that no one else at Toyota could bring the kind of electronics savvy his team did, and the skills were valuable elsewhere if necessary, so he didn't fear for his job.

Furthermore, Peter had worked at Toyota for six years since graduating from college, and had learned that trying to totally fit in to Japanese culture, despite speaking some Japanese and eventually marrying a Japanese woman, wouldn't work.

> I was always a foreigner, always an outsider. I tried too hard, and one day had a kind of a meltdown. I blew up, and said "screw these guys." The Japanese managing director of North America called me in, and I told him why I was frustrated. He said, "If I wanted you to be Japanese I would have hired a Japanese, so stop trying." I was in the first group of U.S. recruits, so we felt all the crap; but it finally worked and they hired more after us.
>
> In college, I worked for ex-president Reagan in his office a year after he finished the presidency; I learned that the old cliché is true: everyone puts his pants on the same way. Guys at the top are lonely SOBs. Reagan was always alone, on a pedestal, which is like all guys at the top. After seeing that every day for a year, I realized Dr. Toyota is not such a big deal, and the president of Toyota USA is just a person. My fear of going up and talking to people was gone.

Without a fancy model of influence, Dames intuitively tuned in to the world of powerful others, and was able to move quickly. In other circumstances, violating a hierarchical culture could lead to termination or banishment, but given his expertise and aspirations and the large number of stakeholders who had to be influenced, it was worth going to the top with a request for the opportunity to show managers what was being proposed rather than just describing it. And Dames realized:

You can't forget that there is a row of people between you and the president; you have to be careful, but we didn't worry about him. I wasn't worried about a job; for example, our business cards were wild. One said: "Better to shoot yourself in the foot than have a competitor shoot you in the head." Our philosophy was "expect to piss people off, push people every day, so go ahead and fire me if you aren't benefiting from our work."

Now, several years later and managing director of PACCAR Financial Europe, Dames tries to remember what it was like as a junior person with ideas, and encourages direct boldness, letting people try their ideas rather than immediately saying no for convenience.

The second example happened to a close colleague, J. Barkev M. Kassarjian (JB as he is known to colleagues and students alike) is a passionate, intense teacher who weaves complex and sophisticated discussions with students, which allows him to know them extremely well. For the last 20 years, JB has split each year between IMD, Lausanne, one of the top business schools in Europe, and Babson College in Massachusetts. His leadership courses are always very highly ranked and alumni name him as having made a memorable impact on their lives.

JB was teaching at IMD in Switzerland and a student noticed that his voice seemed to be much weaker than it was on an earlier videotape where he was interviewing a manager. Pestered to investigate, JB discovered that he had throat cancer. He was treated with radiation at an outstanding Swiss medical center.

For several years there was no recurrence, but a few years ago new malignant growths were discovered. Having already had radiation, there were no good treatment options available, and he was told at a sophisticated prominent cancer treatment center that he would have to go through either a partial or total laryngectomy, which would remove his voice box. Doing his own investigation, JB found that a Dr. Zeitels in Boston (who successfully treated the pop singer Adele) was developing an experimental treatment to starve cancer cells of blood that could be effective. If it worked, he would be spared the laryngectomy operation. His primary care physician, however, could not get an appointment for JB with Dr. Zeitels. The renowned specialist was simply unavailable and JB became frustrated and uncharacteristically despondent.

One evening he was sitting in his office when a former student, Kristen Callahan, appeared in the doorway on her way to another class. She was entrepreneurial and liked to bounce business ideas off of him. This time he was glum, and he asked her to leave. As he recalled, "I muttered, 'Get out of here, I am really pissed at the world.' She asked why, and I must have mentioned Zeitels's name, and I *know* I did not spell it for her."

Kristen later recalled:

JB was lamenting over what road to take with treatment and finally he chose Dr. Z. "I can't even get an appointment with the one doctor I need!" I asked him if he was sure that this was the route he wanted and the guy he wanted. He emphatically replied "YES! He is the best in the world! But I can't get him, no one can. I've tried everything." Once he said that Dr. Z was what he needed, I said to myself, "OK then, that's who it will be.'"

When I left JB's office I searched through my social networks for a tie to Dr. Z, to no avail. Then I researched him online and found his Mass General Hospital and Harvard e-mails buried deep in research papers. Professor Kassarjian taught us to learn to ask forgiveness rather than permission, so I took the initiative and assumed the risk. I considered several means of getting Dr. Z's attention. Personalizing their connection and ties was of utmost importance. I wanted to get past any spam filters he may have for unknown e-mail addresses (most spam is formally addressed), and get his attention in a way that would require him to read on. I finally made the Subject line: "Fellow Harvard PhD desperately needs you." Then I addressed it to "Hi Steven." The message started with: "Before you delete this message, please read the next two sentences." I went on to tell him what an amazing global impact JB has on inspiring future business leaders. I went into the importance to society of his gift, and what an impact his voice, vision, and passion have on shaping socially responsible business leaders. I also mentioned that JB teaches at IMD, which turned out to be another good connection, because he had treated some-one there and knew its importance. Then I tied it back in, putting pressure on him to step up to the plate, to do what he does best and have a measurable impact—globally.

To my amazement, 5 minutes later, still before 6:30 class, my phone rang with a "non-private" number and it was Dr. Z. He asked, "What is all this about?" He said his schedule was full and he could only see JB later in the week. I asked what time he started taking appointments. I then insisted, "How about you see him first thing in the morning, before your first appointment?" He chuckled at my persistence and agreed to see JB before his other appointments the very next day. I then walked back to JB's office, poked my head in his office door and declared, "You have an appointment tomorrow at 7:15 AM, don't be late."

JB was thrilled and amazed that she had found the doctor and been so persuasive that he had agreed. "I would have never addressed him by his first name," JB marveled. "I felt helpless. I am grateful beyond words." (Today, after several surgeries, Kassarjian's voice has been saved, and he has returned to teaching.)

We tell these two stories not because direct approaches always work, but because of the lessons they offer that might help you decide when or if it would be to your advantage to attempt something similar. Peter Dames had learned not to be afraid of senior people or to think of them as totally unapproachable. He had also developed valuable skills, so he did not feel totally dependent on success in his current job. However, he wanted to move things as rapidly as possible. Because he was proposing very radical ideas, he worked hard to show senior man-agers what life could be like if they adopted these exotic sounding (at the time) computer applications.

Kristen Callahan used the power of technology in another way. She tracked down the powerful doctor she wanted to influence using a search function, and plowed through his publications to find an e-mail address. She then thought hard about how to break through e-mail clut-ter and catch his interest. She didn't know that IMD would have mean-ing to him, but correctly deduced that referring to the commonality of a Harvard PhD with his own degrees might intrigue him. Her assumption about addressing him by his first name was extremely astute in that particular context.

Note that both Callahan and Dames each felt that they had little to personally lose. Although that isn't the case for everybody, it does raise the paradox that runs through this book. Worrying extensively about risk decreases your chance of being successful. Before giving up on bold initiatives, ask yourself: "What is the worst thing that could happen?" The worst-case outcome rarely is as catastrophic as you automatically may think. "Premortem analysis" can prevent premature paralysis—or impulsive leaping before looking.

Networking Advice

The same processes you use to gain access to key people are central to identifying who influences your target. What do you likely need from others in your own organization? They may have important information to help you understand more about the senior people you want to influence, useful ideas about how to improve or better present your project, willingness to connect you with key people they know, and sometimes, resources that will help you test or implement your project.

These people might be your peers, or even lower than you in the hierarchy. Wherever they are, you will need to exercise the influence skills and insights presented throughout this book by (1) understanding what matters to them and (2) offering them something valuable in return—whether you explicitly define terms of the exchange or do it just as part of a natural give-and-take process. When you already have a good relationship with people, you may only have to ask—and they will give help if they possibly can. Your ongoing friendship and gratitude may be payment enough—along with the implicit understanding that you will return the favor when needed.

If you have to address someone you don't know very well, recognize that your request may have a cost to the person that you'll have to repay. Are they putting their reputation on the line by vouching for you? If so, there will be expectations of reciprocity. You'll be more likely to get what you need if you create the largest possible network *before* you have specific requests to make. This will increase the possibility that someone you already know can help you—which may then give you access to a powerful person or group.

Unfortunately, many people see networking as a mechanical process. The most important points are (1) know what the people in your network value, so you can help them achieve or gain this; (2) keep track of your connections' activities and accomplishments by using tools like Google News Alerts or LinkedIn.

As you read further, you will see more ways of gaining the access to do the kind of networking described. But it is only when you can get someone's attention that you can build the kind of influential relationship that will make the person willing to respond.

Gaining Access through Active Organizational Involvement That Creates Connections

Most organizations provide at least some opportunities to meet people from other parts of the organization that make it easy to get to know them and their skills. The problem is that many organizational members already feel overloaded with meetings, and avoid these kinds of events and groups. But working with new people is a license to build your network while learning about larger organizational issues. Informal settings can also create chances for new connections, though you will have to move past the interpersonal inertia that slows down many people.

For example, introducing yourself to organizational members and chatting with them about their jobs and experiences can lead to unanticipated connections that are both interesting and potentially valuable. This approach works best when you aren't "in the hunt" for something in particular, and are just interested in getting acquainted. Another option is to interview peers to find out how your area can serve them better, or just to understand what they do. Genuine interest is a wonderful way to start creating a relationship. There's no guarantee that you will ever want anything from these people, but that is all the better for broadening your network and creating currency "credits" that someday you might use.

And high-powered people aren't the only helpful ones. For example, here is what Michael Cummings told us about making connections that were helpful when he was a lower-level manager at John Hancock:

> I have a very friendly relationship with the security guards in our building simply from making an effort to say hello and introduce myself. Because we often receive[d] "secret" visits by those charged with the due diligence, my relationship with the guards allowed me to find out who our visitors were, from where they had arrived, and with whom they had meetings. I anticipated [the] coming acquisition because I was able to get ahead of the curve on understanding Manulife's business.
>
> Another tactic I have found very useful in being prepared to influence upward is something I learned from our former CEO: to always be reading what those on the top are reading. As a result, I subscribe to *Barron's* and other publications that I know our CEO and presidents are reading—information I get from their administrative assistants, other direct reports, and our mailroom manager.

Gaining Access through Gatekeepers

If there are gatekeepers between you and the powerful person, you need to do the same kind of analysis of what they care about as with your final target. What is their world like? How can you give something they value? Are they rewarded for keeping people away? If yes, be explicit about your needs and why you want access. Ask how best to catch the powerful person's attention, what information will be expected, and what medium of communication he or she prefers. Remember, the gatekeeper is a very powerful person in relation to you—so be respectful and understanding of that person's role even if he or she is blocking your path.

In fact, gatekeepers might not only help you get access—they might also be an information source themselves. A scene from the movie *Love and Other Drugs*[2] provides an example of this (perhaps using dramatic license). In the scene, a pharmaceutical sales rep needs an office administrator to get him face time with an incredibly over-scheduled physician. It becomes a contest of ever larger (and unethical if not illegal) gifts to the administrator and then the doctor to ward off a rival sales rep. Though it's a story of reciprocity gone awry, it makes clear that sheer efficacy of drugs may not be enough to get powerful doctors to prescribe—and that getting past the gatekeepers is a constant challenge.

We use this example to illustrate how hard it can be to get past certain kinds of gatekeepers, and therefore how tempting it is to treat relationships as instrumental trades. But make no mistake—even such nice things as just being friendly, connecting around the gatekeeper's interests, and hanging around so long that you can't be ignored are all also forms of currencies. If it turns out none appeal, you won't get an appointment. It isn't manipulative to be genuinely nice, even if you know that it also might be helpful in reaching your goals. In our view, you're manipulating someone only when, if asked, you won't admit your other goals.

Other Methods of Gaining Access

Of course, it may take more imagination on your part to get the first contact with outside senior executives. Only occasionally—in very large companies or bureaucracies—will you need the methods described in "Three Steps to Get a Meeting with Any VP."[3] This widely distributed blog appeared just after the death of Apple chief executive Steve Jobs and recommended donating time to the person's favorite cause, using FedEx for sending your request, using the delivery as an excuse to connect with the person's assistant at the beginning or end of the day, and doing it again if necessary.

When you're trying to reach someone in another organization where you don't have inside help, focus and persistence are required, along with knowledge of how to get your target's attention. You need to think about whether you can find some way to get in his or her orbit—the FedEx letter is one strategy, as previously described. You may need to get their attention just to get *any* sort of response. If they operate in the digital world—via a blog, Facebook, or LinkedIn—follow them wherever you can, then comment frequently until they begin to notice you. People are beginning to learn how vital it is to build an online reputation these days, so that those seeking particular kinds of skills can easily discover you. This is important both within and outside of your own organization.[4]

To identify where your target is engaged in conversation, it is often possible to use certain publicly available programs, such as Klout.com and EmpireState.com. These show you a person's network and where they connect with others. It's also incredibly valuable to approach them in person (at venues like conferences) and ask questions. Someone we know who is good at this calls it "inquiry stalking," a harmless way of getting in a position to eventually connect. What you try to do is ask enough good, exploratory questions to get in the person's peripheral vision, until you are recognized. And often, by reciprocity, you may be asked questions or followed in return. It is even better if you have your own presence and contributions online or in conferences and gatherings such as trade shows and industry events, so that others see you as a person of substance.

For example, Rachel Greenberger is a recent master's of business administration (MBA) graduate with a passion for making a difference about supply-chain issues concerning food and environmental consequences. She did a lot of this kind of electronic and in-person pursuit while looking for job possibilities, but also for connections that could be helpful to her in creating a dream job: starting a food-based organization. She eventually began working with the Lewis Institute for Social Innovation at Babson College (www.babson.edu/Academics/centers/the-lewis-institute/lab/Pages/home.aspx) and helped accomplish the incredibly challenging start-up task of gaining funding for and launching an action project called Food Solutions (Food Sol).

Rachel used social media to gain access to and influence some important players in this space. In the screen shots in Figures 12.1 to 12.3, you can see how she created her own presence on LinkedIn and Twitter, and then connected via these tools with David Stangis, Campbell Soup's vice president for corporate social responsibility (used with permission of both).

You can see how Rachel is making her existence and value known, thereby gaining access to people who are interested in some aspect of food distribution. She finds common ground with others quickly, provides information and connections, and reaffirms each person through her interest while getting to know them. Key people from her industry now follow her tweets and blogs.

FIGURE 12.1 Initial Approach to Dave Stangis by Rachel Greenberger on Twitter

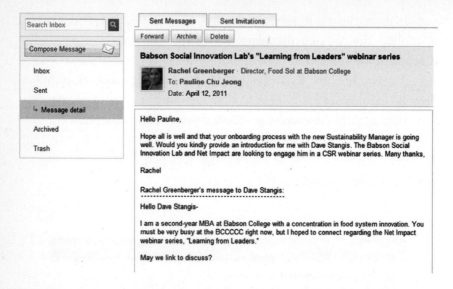

FIGURE 12.2   Initial LinkedIn Connection between Rachel and Dave

FIGURE 12.3   Dave Stangis Communicating via his Twitter Account

Another lesson Rachel teaches us is that you can use social media to get an idea about your target's network. Who do they listen to? Can you gain access from there? Do you know someone who knows them? Can you get an introduction? How about second- or third-degree contacts via LinkedIn? This is a path to borrow someone else's credibility—*if* they are willing to help.

Finding Commonalities

You always want to look for anything that you might have in common with the powerful person—whether it's related to your organization's positions, issues, or even personal interests. For example, is the person on any boards or involved in charitable activities? Is the person's role likely to make for preoccupations with community, country, or world events? Remember—to be instantly credible with a powerful person, you want to be able to connect around larger issues. Although being aware of their personal interest can also work, you will appear relatively closer in power if you can discuss topics related to the powerful person's job. For example, a hot new trend is reverse mentoring, in which young workers advise top managers at places like Hewlett-Packard, Ogilvy & Mather, and Cisco. If one were selected for such an assignment, it would be greatly helpful to know the top manager's interests in advance.[5]

This process takes thought and effort even from a relatively high-power position. Michael May, former head of strategy services at the consulting firm Accenture, describes his experience:

> Put your ego in your back pocket if you are having trouble gaining access, and consider different avenues in. For example—when the [chief operating officer] of U.S. Steel didn't want to see me, I scoured my own organization to find someone with steel industry experience. I finally found one in Japan, and sent him in without me present—thereby completely letting go of my ego. The VP growled at him skeptically, "Have you ever felt the heat of a blast furnace on your cheek?" The Japanese guy turned his head to show his

permanently reddened skin from working in steel mills, and said, "That's why my cheek is so red." The two became instant buddies.

You may not have the equivalent of a steel guy in your hip pocket, but by doing your homework and using your imagination, you may well be able to find some commonality to serve as an opening.

Summary of Overall Access Approach

- **Treat others' views as legitimate, given what they know and perceive—even if they're rejecting you.**

    Surprise the powerful person into looking again by acting as neither an insignificant nobody nor an uppity aspirer—strive to act as a partner. You are trying to pique the person's interest just long enough to exchange at least another sentence or two. If you can do this, you might be able to get a conversation going another time—possibly even an instant reassessment about how worthwhile it would be to pay attention to you.

    If you get a dismissive response, that is exactly the critical moment at which to be thinking like a partner, saying to yourself, "This person doesn't yet see the benefits of what I want to talk about; but since it will be for the good of the organization and him or her, I need to come at this another way. Of course, I might need to tweak my offer in some way as well." Maintaining this attitude over time can help you earn enough respect to be able to engage with the person.

- **Deliver valuable currencies—before the other person asks for anything.**

    Analyze whether there is anything valuable you can deliver before you request something of this person, and possibly even before you have had any direct contact.

    When access is a problem, ask others for ideas of what might be valuable. Then do the work, and see if there is anyone likely to be interested in what you have done—and might tell your target about it. Is the company facing new competition? Are there new laws that could make things difficult? What will the impact be of new attention on sustainability? If you can pick something to study that crosses areas, then there is less risk of being seen as an interloper—and more chance of being perceived as helpful. You have to address the issues in an impartial way that can make action easier for senior decision makers.

- **Adjust your style to the preferences of the powerful person's style.**

    This rule always applies when you are interacting with a powerful person, and is especially true when approaching a distant one. The style you use can make a big difference when you get only a very brief shot with someone who doesn't know you. Does he or she prefer openness, brevity, warmth, formal distance, overt respect, task or relationship first, data or proposal first? We believe in what we call the 15 percent rule: be just a little more open, or direct, or vulnerable than the other party expects. Not so much that it makes the person uncomfortable, but slightly more than he or she might expect from a stranger. This may require being tougher, blunter, more concise, more deferential, or something else that isn't automatic for you. But usually you will have it somewhere in your repertoire.

    It might be worth thinking about why style and even superficial things like clothing and appearance matter so much. The higher one's position in an organization, the more one has to deal with uncertainty and ambiguity, and the more one has to make decisions that have long-term consequences. Because relevant and genuine expertise is therefore hard to judge, people below or from outside often are judged by whether they appear to be sufficiently similar to the senior person.

    The next step in enhancing your influence is to increase your own power, which has already begun as part of gaining access. But there is more to examine—which we do in the next chapter.

CHAPTER

13

Clinching the Deal

"Exchanging" to Build Trust with the Powerful

You found a way to get to the table. And although you might have reduced the power gap between you and the other party, it still exists. What are you going to do to gain at least some of what you want while building a more trusting relationship at the same time?

You don't want to be forceful or dominating, or to bluff. It can be difficult to balance your role as a potential junior partner without seeming presumptuous or arrogant; presumptions of superiority won't work when power differences are obvious.

There may even be times when you have such little power that all you can do is throw yourself at the mercy of the powerful party's good will and essentially pay back in gratitude. However, this approach leaves you dependent and powerless—a situation with poor long-term prospects. It is in your own and the organization's interest to build the exchange process toward mutuality, making maximum contributions

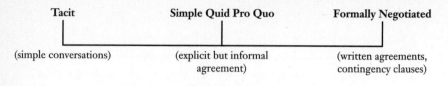

FIGURE 13.1   Range of Influence Exchanges

and solving problems creatively. The illustration in Figure 13.1 and the following discussion describe how you can conduct yourself in a way that will prompt others to take you seriously and hear you out—even if you have to come back another time to do it.

Exchanges can happen anywhere; you rarely even notice you're making them with close and relatively equal colleagues. If you need something, you ask, and vice versa, and each helps the other out. Payback is frequently taken for granted during the course of most daily work. But as power distance increases, you must look at these conversations as negotiations with the person you want to influence, because you cannot assume that the other side is willing to cooperate. It's also fair to assume that it's up to you to prove that you can deliver valued currencies (such as return on investment [ROI], enhanced organizational reputation, greater market share, or whatever is valued by the decision makers) in return for what you're asking. Quid pro quo is likely to be the starting place.

It's also a good idea to determine your fallback position, the minimum influence and/or the maximum "price" you can accept before walking away. This is called BATNA in negotiations—the "best alternative to a negotiated agreement." Although your interaction may not be this formal, it helps to know what you'll accept.

Dual Focus: Determining What You Want and Constantly Improving the Relationship

There are always two things at play during an exchange: the specific contents that are at stake and the nature of the relationship as the exchange unfolds. In general, it is better for your potential outcome to enhance trust and openness during any discussion, because this also increases the long-term benefits to you and the organization.

If you are bringing a proposal from below in the organization, you will almost inevitably have to work your way up through the formal hurdles and gating process, and informal barriers from individuals or units. There will inevitably be some in the organization who want to stop or dramatically change what you want; maybe they don't understand it, or believe—accurately or not—that implementation would make their lives more difficult somehow.

Therefore, we advocate for a few ironclad laws of organizational influence:

- **Listen to everyone, including the most ardent opponents.** Even if you do not change your approach, showing them that you'll listen seriously might prompt them to be less opposed— and might even yield good ideas for modification that can gain support.

- **Don't leave a discussion unless the other party thinks better of you personally.** You want to demonstrate not only competence, but also genuine respectfulness of differing views. That enhances your reputation and will help you as you move up the hierarchy. If managers along the way speak well of you, the most powerful are more likely to want to hear from you.

- **Do not ignore your original supporters; reinforce your relationships so that you don't lose them.** It's natural to take for granted those who are automatic beneficiaries of what you propose, and those who think first about organizational benefits rather than personal ones. Keep them informed and encouraged.

Except for when you are dealing exclusively with your natural allies, you will face considerable challenges when seeking influence; the challenges are due to what we have come to call the "negotiating influencer's paradox." There is considerable research evidence to suggest that the best deals are created—those with value for both sides— when all interests and goals are on the table. The more open both people are, the easier it is to creatively satisfy their interests. Zero sum win-lose is seldom the case in organizational issues. Even in situations where two people are competing for something, it is a good idea to think about preserving relationships because of the potential for future interactions.

The paradox, however, is if trust does not already exist, it would be naïve to put all your cards on the table immediately. That leaves you too vulnerable to an opponent who wants to take advantage of you. Of course, the other party doesn't want to go first either—which makes it difficult to start with complete openness.

The goal is to initiate the relationship in a way that builds trust and openness. The starting point is to be certain that you are speaking to the other party's interests, and especially for senior people, organizational benefits. Although there is often an overlap, the organizational benefits may not be identical to the powerful person's individual best interest, and you need to be alert to those personal interests as they emerge in discussion, and eventually address them. Nevertheless, not only is the benefit to the organization likely to be an important currency, but it raises the level of the discussion. Without this other-centered guiding focus, not much else matters.

Don't forget to take into account the way in which people prefer to be related to. In general, powerful people prefer concise and direct presentations that begin with the conclusions and an overall sense of the benefits proposed. A technical consultant to entrepreneurial engineers told us recently about how frustrating it was to help them prepare for pitches to potential funding sources. He would constantly emphasize the need to just present the benefits, and would then watch in horror as one after another immediately launched into deep dives about the science behind their product—causing eyes to glaze over within minutes.

A good proposal concisely describes the problem that needs to be solved, how the proposed product or service solves it, how the plan will make or save money compared to the costs of implementation, the key assumptions behind the plan, and the downside risks with fallback plans, leaving everything else to be answered only if there are questions. (See the later section "Even in Japan, It Is Possible to Influence Powerful People" for an illustration of this phenomenon.)

Addressing the Power Gap

By now, you have done your homework and are presenting your topic with appropriate expertise. You must be—and appear—confident, and not get written off before you even get started. This is a complex challenge, one that Michael May, former global managing partner of the strategy service line at Accenture, conceptualizes as having to *come across as a peer, but not appear arrogant.* According to May, "You need to have these personal influence resources to be seen as a peer, with 'non-arrogant peerism.'" That is, you need to relate as equals no matter the level of the other person. According to May, the "personal influence resources" are:

1. A sense of self-worth and personal value
2. Interpersonal skills
3. Ability to think critically [Perhaps most important for a strategy consultant, but hardly irrelevant for any aspiring influencer.]
4. A visible thought process, where the other person can see how you conceptualize and analyze the issues
5. Optimized communication, adjusted to fit the receptivity of the other person

May goes on to elaborate on these dimensions:

- Self-worth

  I had a project with Northwestern Mutual early in my career where I had to deal with a manager from hell; he cut everyone off before they spoke, always knew the answer. We had a project review; after scanning a page or two, he literally ripped my report in half: "You call yourself a consultant, go make it better!" The next time after two weeks more work, he did it again. He was screaming at me; I snapped. "Don't you scream at me that way, I deserve more respect than that." He smiled and said, "I was waiting for that. I have a conference room set aside for us, let's go talk." I believed in my worth enough to stand up to him when I thought we had done our work well.

You have to reflect on what is called for while staying true to yourself. And you have to be at or above the energy level of the other.

- Interpersonal skill for nonarrogant peerism

  You have to understand the individual you are trying to influence to the greatest degree you can. If it is someone who started in the mailroom and worked his or her way up, or was brought in from outside over others, what do they deal with every day? Suppose it is a 30-year veteran, an experiential-base manager; what sort of individual would you bring with you to the meeting? Whatever the individual's situation or experience, you have to change what you do each time according to this, and relate uniquely to their experience.

  People who fail to act as peers ask no questions about the business, or use "Mr." with a CEO (although this is cultural; in some countries you have to, but in the U.S. it puts him above you). Saying, "I know you are extremely busy," lowers you. Don't lead with your business card; if the person doesn't know who you are by the end of the meeting, it won't matter whether you've given it to them or not. And always, always make eye contact.

- Critical thinking

  Make sure you identify the other person's playing field, and how important the topic is to them. Try to figure out their top concerns in that territory, then construct a situation or example so real that they deal with it all the time. Can you capture their frustrations? What are the reasons they get pushback? You might not have a solution, but you demonstrate familiarity with the issue.

However, let's suppose you read it wrong or didn't figure out the biggest challenges for that person during your preparation. One-to-one discussion works best if you already have a relationship, because it usually prompts the other person to be open more quickly. Bring someone else along whose style differs from yours if you do not know the person; this allows two people to serve as a sounding board.

For example, I had a sales meeting with the Merrill Lynch CEO Dave Komansky, a long-term McKinsey client. I began by trying to relate to him like a McKinsey partner, which didn't reflect who he was. As it turned out, he is more of a family guy and is very indirect. I saw my assumption was wrong, stopped, and quickly shifted gears by saying, "You might prefer me to get down to more specifics." He smiled, and then we talked. You have to be willing to let go of your own agenda.

First you have to recognize you took the wrong direction, then get them talking so you can learn.

- Visible thought process

I happen to like the issue-based problem-solving method, a cascading decision tree that starts by asking: What questions have to be answered to address a major problem? This allows the other to see your process. "The major problem is X." . . . Next, "The four to five major causes are A, B, C, D . . . Finally, "The data which lets us conclude that is . . ." Being clear about how you will tackle the problem helps build credibility.

- Optimized communication

Some people wonder whether they should be direct or indirect in addressing the issue at hand. Start with irrefutable facts if you don't expect your target to be receptive, and then move to a conclusion. If they are receptive, explain the opportunity, and then only go as deep as you need to. The simpler someone speaks, the more impact they have.

I always make sure that I know the top five issues this person is facing. I want a conversation, not an interview; that means possibly fewer topics, but more back and forth, even with a bit of disagreement. You want fewer questions, and deeper content. Top people see too many "yes men"; few challenge them, or push outside the conventional boundaries. You earn respect as a peer by having an informed view on the critical issues. Be sure to disagree without attacking. Tie what you say to the large problems with which they're concerned.

I have no problem saying "I don't understand this area. Let me get someone who does."

Other Strategies for Increasing Your Power with Senior Management in Your Own Organization

We have already emphasized linking to organizational goals, and using every discussion as an opportunity to learn more about how to shape your proposal. As careful as you've diagnosed this person's world—pressures, needs, currencies—that is still a working hypothesis that you might have to instantly change. You have the opportunity to continuously test, during interactions, whether your understanding of their world and their concerns is accurate. However, make sure you test in a way in which you are not making a CLM (career-limiting move) or creating a negative self-fulfilling prophecy.

For example, keep tying your points to the problems that will be solved, and check whether this connection is clear. You are essentially saying, "This recommendation is intended to (prevent suffering, avoid loss of customers, reduce wasteful expenditures, etc.); are the connections clear or do you need to hear more evidence?" This leaves room to gracefully retreat, and is likely to be a lot less threatening than a statement that implies the target of your influence pitch is an idiot for propagating existing practices.

Remember too that executives have both common and differing concerns. Though they have the organization's overall benefit as a priority, they're each in charge of a distinct area with differing subgoals, measures, and preoccupations. This is why it's best to meet or at least gather data from each; this will allow you to address those concerns or do so before presenting. It's also helpful to discern whether the group *really* makes joint decisions, or defers on all important matters to the top person. The more you know about these dynamics, the less chance that your lack of knowledge will cause the other person to have an exaggerated view of your lower-power status.

Another related point is that you should never assume bad intentions of anyone in the organization, whether explicitly or implicitly. Assume everyone wants to do the best, and cares about overall results for customers, the public, and external stakeholders (including stockholders or other financing groups). But they may not have seen the unintended consequences of the existing practice or process. This is a variation of not falling in love with your approach (or technology) for its own sake, but of connecting your proposal to desirable and identifiable outcomes.

Try to see objections or tough questions as useful statements of others' currencies. Then find a way to speak to these—accepting their right to have different currencies and paying them in those—rather than trying to talk them out of it. You are more of a peer if you are working from these premises, believing that other smart people can value quite different things, yet be open to cooperating with something that will do ultimate good.

Just as in other negotiations, always be prepared if necessary to settle for intermediate outcomes that will provide movement toward your ultimate goal. When Peter Dames was trying to create a completely new and unheard of electronic environment for Toyota cars (as described in Chapter 12), he knew that a first step would be to create a way for executives to become familiar with what might be possible. So he worked at getting a demonstration lab where they could see simple applications and play with the technology. He realized he couldn't get all the way to his ultimate goal directly. You'll often take two steps forward and one back in a large, complex organization—and you need to persist while adapting along the way.

Connecting to Frequently Important Personal Currencies

Given the obligations and pressures under which senior executives work—coupled with the fact that they might be the only person focused on those concerns—many tend to feel separate or misunderstood by those below. If you can use your diagnosis of their world to connect with them, you'll increase your apparent "peerness" and credibility. It can be something as simple as making a comment tied to a current news event about which they're concerned. You don't have to be the expert or agree with the executive; you just have to show that you are aware of the forces acting on them, think about such issues, and can converse about them like a peer.

Another domain in which you may have important knowledge or "expertise" is your awareness of the way this powerful person's behavior impacts those below. How do employees perceive his or her decisions? Did the memo about the new strategy make a dent in the organization, or would more follow-up be useful? Did the declaration about the need for more innovation inspire or bewilder the troops? The valuable knowledge you have adds to your power.

Because you don't want it to seem like you're criticizing, be very careful about how you introduce this valuable (but potentially explosive) information. Always assume the best of intentions, and link your comment with the powerful person's goals (it is the *means* that you are raising the questions about). Connect your input to the need to solve the core problem being addressed, and suggest extra effort to be sure it is achieved. This approach conveys that you both care about the results and want to achieve them better, faster, or more completely. Not only does this approach allow you to reduce the power gap, but it also helps cure low-power laryngitis, because it provides a way to speak up without attacking or implying incompetence.

Because confirmation of their power is a very common currency of the powerful, never be afraid to let the powerful person teach you, and feel important as a result. It takes strength and confidence to let someone share their expertise with you without having to prove yourself smart and knowledgeable—or playing dumb. Showing off your smarts isn't the same as letting it come through in your attentiveness, ability to listen, learn, admire expertise, and appreciate the willingness of the other to share knowledge.

If the powerful person is teaching something that you already know—either in an attempt to make you feel or look small, or simply because he or she doesn't know that you're already familiar with this— resist the need to retaliate or show off. You can mention after listening that you have some knowledge in this area; ask some questions, or cover another topic where the person can show off. Besides, listening carefully will teach you important lessons about the person's currencies, and probably compel him or her to listen to you sooner or later.

As in any negotiation, don't try to win every point. Consider everything the other person has said before settling any issues; the more issues that are in play, the greater the chance to come up with creative solutions. This also allows you more latitude to give on things that don't matter as much to you in order to preserve what matters most. That's why it isn't terrible to have a powerful person raise many objections to your proposal or request; it lets you understand the territory and achieve good trade-offs. Besides, listening carefully to concerns and objections is a kind of payment of respect in its own right, and can create a bit of reciprocal willingness to hear you out.

Finally, meet the other where he or she is in terms of preferred style. If they like to be tough, hang in and be a worthy adversary. Allow them to feel big and important if they like that; don't focus on proving how worthy you are. Peers don't worry about proving themselves; they just work from where the partner is and let the proof be in the give and take.

Where You Have Little Relationship and Trust Is Low

In situations where you have little connection and trust—for example, you're dealing with a poor track record or new people—one good strategy is to offer to deliver a lot before expecting any return.

This makes you more vulnerable and might require using "sweat equity," where you put in extra hours or divert regular resources to demonstrate that you're willing to take risks without asking for much in return. Just be clear about what you are doing, so that the other person sees it as positive.

It might be possible to make guarantees, or agree on penalties if you don't deliver. You'll also want to agree on how to monitor progress, decide on checkpoints, and figure out relevant measures. Powerful people have been known to grant a shot to a person or team that shows real persistence and imagination in risking themselves, and who are willing to be closely monitored. Remember the informal product development team in Chapter 1 that overspent $6 million without permission, and went to a senior manager with all the financials and their rationale for predicting a valuable business opportunity, and offered to let him monitor everything they spent going forward? That they had a compelling story helped, but so did their willingness to informally report to the senior executive, have him track their progress, and stop their work at any time.

The process of trying to influence the most powerful person or group is a high-stakes proposition; however, there's more involved than just gaining that person's cooperation. Getting turned down may or may not be the true end; chances are that your experience has taught you how to make necessary modifications for another round. It's also likely to have enhanced your reputation for whatever influence attempts you make in the future. As hard as you try to get short-term positive results, remember that we are all almost always playing for the long term.

Even in Japan, It Is Possible to Influence Powerful People

The information in this section is from interviews with Yasuhiro Yamamoto, translation by Kaoru and Naruhide Takashima.

The characteristics of skillful influencers are remarkably similar, even across cultures. Yasuhiro Yamamoto, 46, is a professional marketer and consultant and the president of Business Value Creations, Inc. He started his career in a traditional Japanese beverage company, and in his late twenties created big hit beverages including a new type of vegetable juice mixed with fruits named "Jujitsu-Yasai." He also developed successful products in other companies. He recounted how he managed to be influential with powerful people throughout his career's history. His reasoning and behavior are quite consistent with the practices advocated in this book.

He had joined a company at the age of 33 where he noticed a product plan for a PET-plastic bottled green tea that he thought was "rubbish." There was no known demand and unpleasant taste, and many employees were unhappy about it. He decided to design a different product as a way of stopping the green tea. He created a complete business plan and proceeded to approach everyone related to product development that might support him.

He presented his plan to a colleague in the marketing department to get a sense of possible responses in the company. He then won over sales people and the chief of the sales department by getting their opinions—a tactic that made them feel involved in product planning, and that they had created it together. He focused on the conditions at supermarkets and convenience stores, because their interests and situations were different. Both sales reps were grateful because Yamamoto knew both kinds of outlets from his past experience and was able to show the plan's connections to each.

His next step was to get the general manager to his side, for which Yamamoto changed his approach totally. He didn't mention the product's features, but instead presented the business scheme with action steps to achieve the related goals given the market data and figures. Yamamoto was finally able to get an

(*continued*)

(continued)

opportunity to present to the director in charge of product development. It took him several rounds to persuade the director, and he then received 90 days to realize the product, from a sketch to a real (prototype) product. He aggressively carried out the new plan; due to the support that sales gave him, he was promoted to the chief of the marketing department. This newfound position allowed Yamamoto to reach completion more aggressively, in 90 days as promised. After completion, the premarket screening was conducted to compare two products, his and the initial one. The result was his product's overriding win.

Yamamoto was a keen student of higher management. For example, when he heard the product development director talking about ordering his suits from a British Savile Row tailor, he said "Oh, then I'm going to order my suits, too! I definitely need a real suit by Savile Row for promotional events of the product, new product presentations." The director warned him that a single suit cost 300,000 yen (more than $3,000) and asked Yamamoto if he was comfortable buying such expensive suits. Yamamoto replied, "Of course; the company pays me enough to afford that!"

Further, Yamamoto decided to interact with members of the management board by observing their preferred methods of responding. As a result, they took him under their wings and treated him kindly. For example, one day he noticed at a meeting that the director who approved Yamamoto's plan jiggled his legs when he was being told anything he did not think important, but stopped when hearing something he was interested in. Yamamoto concluded that this person was sure about what he would like to hear, and liked to be told it directly. So—counter to typical Japanese organizational style—Yamamoto gave his conclusion first, and explained the details only when the explanation was asked. This served him well. Soon after, Yamamoto saw one of the general managers starting to go into details in one meeting, which prompted the senior director's legs to start jiggling.

Just when Yamamoto noticed, the director asked Yamamoto for his opinion about the issue. Yamamoto replied directly with the conclusion. The senior director was glad to hear that directness, and said "Good, good! I'll take that. Go for what Yamamoto-kun said." After this incident, the senior director began to ask Yamamoto's thoughts first.

The higher a person gets in an organization, the more problems he gets to deal with—and the less time he has. This means that the high-powered person needs to hear conclusions much more quickly.

Yamamoto used his understanding of what senior people cared about and how they preferred information to get to the bottom line quickly, and rapidly gained influence. He has used his ability to tune in to the currencies of others to create a highly successful marketing/consulting business at a younger age than is customary in Japan.

We have now covered the core of what you need to influence very powerful people. In the last two chapters, we provide rich illustrations of how a doctor and a retired woman each used all the influence elements to tackle complex, multi-stakeholder situations against overwhelming odds and managed to achieve their goals.

14

The Contours of Change

Dr. Pomahac and the Challenge of Influencing Multiple Senior Managers and Surgeons to Allow the First Facial Transplant in the United States

Background: The Need

It would be very difficult to find a more challenging influence project than the one undertaken by Dr. Bohdan Pomahac of Boston's Brigham and Women's Hospital. A young plastic surgeon, he had been treating a patient whose face had been so badly burned and disfigured that he wouldn't even leave the house. The Doctor knew that no matter how much reconstructive surgery he did, the net effect would never be acceptable.

Dr. Pomahac had been following the articles and discussions about the possibility of facial transplants. When a French team actually did the first one in November 2005, he resolved to find a way to do it himself. He knew that they not only replace what is missing for the patient; they can truly transform lives. The challenge would be to overcome the resistance of his own department, senior surgeons, large teams of doctors and nurses, and the regional organ donor agency that would have to find families willing to donate a deceased family member's face. He'd also have to persuade elite surgeons to let him take the face first (endangering the removal of organs they were waiting for), and then raise millions of dollars to pay for not only the surgery but the lifelong course of immunosuppression drugs that would be needed. Each step could be a major influence hurdle in its own right; taken together, they seemed insurmountable. He spent more than three years gaining acceptance and support.

We first learned about Dr. Pomahac from a splendid feature article in the *Boston Globe*[1] that outlined many of the individuals and groups he had to influence. He graciously agreed to fill us in on his thinking and methods.

Dr. Pomahac's story is so important because he combines an intuitive feel for what matters to people whose cooperation he needs with an analytical ability to think through the steps required to achieve his goals. The senior surgeons he approached at his teaching hospital advised him to follow the traditional route: lay out a laboratory research plan and do the investigations and publishing that would prove the methods and value of facial transplants. Because Dr. Pomahac knew that process would take about 10 years, and patients were suffering deep social isolation, he thought about the possibility of reverse engineering: doing a facial transplant or two and using *that* as the start of the backup research in his lab and possibly elsewhere. This was an option because there were no new and unproven technologies involved; it wouldn't require Food and Drug Administration approval. Though facial transplants were incredibly complex, the microsurgery, technology, and immunosuppression were already well established with other kinds of transplants. No one had put it all together.

Until the French announcement, facial transplants were a "hobby project" for Dr. Pomahac. His main efforts as an attending physician were to set up a laboratory and a series of experiments in cartilage engineering. That was proving to be extraordinarily difficult, with crazy hours and "slow, pathetic progress." So he set out to find another senior surgeon who might support him.

Finding Allies

He soon discovered two interested senior surgeons: Dr. Elof Eriksson, chief of plastic surgery and the man who had originally allowed him to do unpaid lab work at the hospital, and Dr. Julian Pribaz, a renowned surgeon. Because Pribaz was very progressive, independent, and not afraid to try new things, he turned out to be a perfect ally. But he had no time to be directly involved, so he just encouraged Dr. Pomahac—and truly believed that he could pull it off.

Dr. Pomahac followed a strategy wherein he did all the work but gave everyone else the credit. He knew that if a huge project like this one went wrong, it could end his career. But Dr. Pomahac intuitively thought this was the right project to bet on. The support of both senior doctors turned out to be very important.

Overcoming Institutional Objections

As Dr. Pomahac saw it, the big issue was how to put all the pieces together. The hospital had an institutional review board (IRB) that had to approve the project, which could take a long time; that same process for face transplants had taken 10 years in a comparable hospital in Cleveland. Additionally, the hospital had to come up with funding to get the project underway. No one had been to the organ bank, whose cooperation was needed to find donors. Dr. Pomahac reasoned,

"If I get everyone involved early on, they will feel a part of the process and more sympathetic. Personal contact is critical to move beyond the formal processes." He reached out to the IRB chair and brought some very dramatic before and after pictures of the French patient. He explained what he wanted to do, cited why he thought it was important, and asked for her advice about the best way to handle the process. She only gave him the rules for how to submit for approval, which would have happened for anyone who wanted to apply; however, she seemed moved by the discussion.

He went on to do the same thing at the New England Organ Bank. He gave their board (and four separate groups of transplant surgeons) a presentation on the topic, but he had the sense that they were suspicious that he was doing this only to boost his ego. As a result, he never pressured anyone to rush the process; he was always sure to put the patient's interests first. The board offered to set him up to meet with their consortia meeting every three months. Dr. Pomahac sensed that they were testing him, so he let them take their time in order to make sure that it would never seem that he was personally trying to win a race. He recognized inwardly that though being the first in the United States would be nice and probably help attract funding, it was best to keep coming back to potential life-changing benefits for patients.

A Complex Integrated Plan—and Real Time Corrections

Dr. Pomahac then started the long process of writing everything up and bringing all the details together. He had to answer two substantial questions: (1) Because no one had done the operation before, how should it be designed in order to surgically make it happen? and (2) How could they get a donor? If the family coordinators at the organ bank wouldn't ask families, it just wouldn't happen. Because there is great emotion attached to the notion of giving up a face for a transplant, it was hard to imagine making the request—so this became a key element upon which Dr. Pomahac was forced to spend time. It was controversial and encompassed concerns about whether the recipient would look exactly like the donor, creating possibly awkward encounters with the family, and concerns about how to pay for a lifetime of immunosuppression drugs.

Dr. Pomahac's strategy was to create the first protocol in a way that would eliminate all controversy. He suggested that they only do a partial face transplant to completely demonstrate that it would not transfer identity. As he explained:

> We knew it shouldn't happen, but to definitely show it, we proposed using a partial face, where even someone who worked with the person day-to-day wouldn't recognize the original person's face. We actually designed and published a study on this. Then we proposed picking patients who were already on the drugs because they had some other transplant to deal with immunosuppression.
>
> This would be a perfect population that not only knew about risks and benefits of life on immunosuppression, but also did not represent any additional cost of drugs that would remain the same.

Outside Influences

As it happened, despite no planning for it, there was considerable media interest in facial transplants, a topic that apparently hooks widespread audiences. This turned out to be useful in reducing resistance among those that had to be convinced to cooperate, because good press serves to familiarize and legitimize unusual major changes.

Even with the improved protocol, some people at the hospital whose approval was needed were still hesitant to do so. Because chief of surgery Dr. Michael Zinner was reluctant to give the go-ahead, Dr. Pomahac's supporter, Dr. Eriksson, came up with a wonderful idea: Dr. Joseph Murray, a Nobel laureate who had performed the world's first kidney transplant at the Brigham in 1954, was being honored. Eriksson suggested inviting Dr. Max Dubernard, who had done the world's first hand transplant and was part of the face team in France. Dubernard had been a fellow in Murray's lab 40 years ago. An extremely charismatic and colorful person, he came to the Brigham and showed a video of the first patient with the hand transplant, playing a game of pickup sticks and then threading a needle, and another of the first face patient talking and smiling. No one had ever seen these videos, and all were amazed and moved. Then at the actual dinner, without prompting, Dr. Dubernard, during his speech, turned to Dr. Zinner and loudly declared, "Facial transplants are the future and you have to support them!" This of course helped move Zinner to become more supportive.

In the meantime, the restrictive protocol for patients with existing other transplants was not yielding any patients. Dr. Pomahac then had to persuade hospital officials to open the surgery to any badly disfigured patients. As they set about to select the first patient, he presented the original patient with the horribly burned face, Jim Maki, whose case had been so frustrating to him. There was a great deal of skepticism about whether Jim was the right choice; the entire surgical division was in the room, and the more willing junior people found it hard to convince the experienced practitioners. It took a lot of support from Eriksson and Pribaz to gain approval.

Dr. Pomahac did a conservative estimate of the cost and realized that probably no one would pick up the lifetime costs of the immunosuppression drugs. Working with the office of the physicians practice group that daily dealt with insurance companies, they managed to come to the following agreement: they would pick up the expense three months after the surgery. It turned out that language in the Medicare law generically said that drug costs would be covered "for suppressing rejection" but did not specify particular transplant organs, so facial transplants qualified. Each proposed patient requires a new approval process, but it becomes possible.

The hospital board then had to agree to pay for the first patient's procedure and hospital stay. They were persuaded to go forward and to negotiate with Medicaid for the needed ongoing drugs. Chances are that the growing approvals and buzz prompted the willingness to go ahead.

Remembering Less Prominent but Still Important Stakeholders

Dr. Pomahac still had to do a bit more follow-up work with the family coordinators from the organ bank; unless he was able to genuinely convince them, they would never be able to persuade a donor's family to cooperate. Dr. Pomahac went to visit them three more times, bringing along pictures and giving them extra time and attention. He worked to make them see that it would never be able to happen without them; he believed that the combination of the powerful pictures and letting them feel that they were important made a difference. He knew they had to share the vision. At first they would only approach a family who they thought would be open to the possibility—but that was almost no one. However, they've become comfortable with the prospect and are willing to ask any donor family. It also helps that Jim Maki is doing remarkably well.

Conclusions

It only takes a little bit of reading between the lines to recognize that Dr. Pomahac's combination of intuition and analytical skills worked together to make him particularly effective. His experience as a chess player allowed him to see all the components that needed to be linked together and develop a reasonable sequence to follow. He was persistent in achieving his overall goal, but showed considerable flexibility in adapting what had to be done to get there. He also developed an excellent sense of what mattered to the different stakeholders, and combined methodical attention to detail with a clear eye on the ultimate prize.

Although Dr. Pomahac is ambitious, he was keenly aware any hint of this ambition might make some senior medical people less willing to cooperate. He needed to show them that his primary goal was to do what was right for patients, who were asking for the procedure despite the complications and risks. He noticed that people who might be considered less important than the doctors—like the family coordinators who had to recruit donors—also needed to feel that they were contributing to a grand vision. He recognized that personal contact was as important as bureaucratic procedure, and he made personal connections while carefully following recognized organizational requirements.

When confronted with skeptical surgeons and other doctors who were used to following systematic and deliberate research procedures, Dr. Pomahac used the vivid pictorial examples to transcend the abstractions. He showed how individuals had been unable to live visible, public lives until the transplants that allowed them to be fully human again. He didn't put down the doctors' commitment to research, nor his own long-term commitment to it; he simply proved that early adoption of the procedures could stimulate research, speaking to currencies both valued. Making a vision memorable can transcend considerable resistance.

Although this example is written in terms of the actions he took as a world class influencer, Dr. Pomahac certainly benefited from the efforts of many—"a little help from his friends"—and some good fortune on which he was then able to capitalize. He managed to influence some powerful individuals, and convince them of his deep care for alleviating the miseries of patients. When people believed that about him, they were more willing to help.

So far, four fortunate facial transplant patients have been the beneficiaries of Dr. Pomahac's skill, determination, and focus, and he has helped advance an important medical, identity-saving process. It is only fitting that he was featured in the hospital's year-end fund-raising appeal, and on the cover of the December 2011 issue of *Boston Magazine*, which highlighted "Top Docs and Amazing Medical Breakthroughs from 2011."

CHAPTER

15

Influence across Multiple Organizations

It is difficult enough to influence one powerful person, but trying to impact a high-powered group is even more complicated. The true challenge is in having to sway members of many different organizations—often with very different agendas—in a similar direction. Everything we have discussed about using a partnership mind-set, diagnosing highly varied and sometimes imperceptible currencies, finding something useful to offer in exchange for what is needed, comes into play.

To help you see how this can all come together, we introduce you to Barbara Spangler, who took on a monumental and demanding project in her community with multiple stakeholders. She succeeded by using a combination of already developed skills, learning along the way, and summoning the courage to do what was needed even when it was personally uncomfortable for her.

After she retired from GE Healthcare, where she had served as a bridge builder between university researchers and corporate engineering designers in interventional cardiology, Barbara wanted to do something useful with her new freedom. While she was exploring ideas, she found herself in the middle of an opportunity to practice making something complex and valuable happen. In fact, the project ended up becoming so complex that Barbara decided to add to her skills and knowledge by entering a master's of business administration (MBA) program. Massachusetts-based Babson College had launched a hybrid MBA in nearby San Francisco with an entrepreneurial focus that was part face to face and part online. That's how we met her.

She was living in Oakmont Village within Santa Rosa, California, serving as president of the Oakmont Golf Club. Her role there led her to become aware of a threat by the city of Santa Rosa to shut down the wastewater treatment plant that had been built by the golf club almost 50 years ago. It had been deeded along with a major portion of property taxes to Santa Rosa in return for permanent maintenance, free water supply, and normal city services. The city had recently built a modern, high-capacity wastewater treatment plant roughly 20 miles away. However, the city was strapped for budget funds and was planning to break its agreement, close the Oakmont wastewater plant, and stop delivering free water for irrigation of the golf course.

This would have cost golf club members heavily, and it wasn't clear whether or not it would even be legal. Board and club members who heard the rumors were ready to hire lawyers and do battle with the city; however, Barbara argued for a different approach. Barbara had come across Robert Axelrod's *The Evolution of Collaboration* early in her career, a book that used game theory to show how tit-for-tat strategy usually prompted one's opponent to collaborate. Personally sunny and optimistic, she was committed to using a more partnerlike approach in all of her dealings:

> I approach people with the intent to cooperate. I assume the best of everyone, all the time, unless I'm proven otherwise. I've found that is the way to get the best out of everyone. I frame interactions

by creating a supportive environment in which subordinates, colleagues, and superiors all give more.

After checking with a lawyer and learning that the golf club might well have a defensible contract, she persuaded her more feisty colleagues on the board that a potential standoff would cost a fortune in legal fees—not to mention the painful process they'd have to endure. She reminded them that the expense would affect them either way as city residents. When one antagonistic board member claimed that he didn't have the time for this endeavor, Barbara explained that she did—and was willing to invest in the process. Barbara saw a great deal of obtainable help, because the community had some very smart members. They could have retired anywhere, but decided to be in Oakmont Village. The other members knew based on her history that Barbara could get things done—and so they all went along.

Key Players

It helps to have a scorecard to track the players in a complicated project like this one. In all, the project required agreement from more than 40 people. The five main groups involved were the Oakmont Golf Club, the Oakmont Village Association (OVA, governing body of Oakmont community), the Oakmont Property Development Committee (OPDC, a subcommittee of the OVA established to advise on matters pertaining to land development and potential government ordinances), and the Santa Rosa Board of Public Utilities (representing the city). A negotiating committee was also selected on behalf of the golf club, with joint membership from the golf club and the village; the city also appointed two active members, for a total of eight, and named the director and vice chair of public utilities as secondary members.

One source of tension early in the process was the somewhat strained historical relationship between the golf club and the village. It hadn't always been exactly clear what the relationship was supposed to be like, because the golf club membership represented a large portion of the village population, but not all. Association members paid a monthly fee that did not include any maintenance for the golf courses, even though they were a large part of the attractive land of the village. Barbara immediately offered to appear before a village board meeting to brief all the property owners on the current state of the wastewater situation. This allowed the village association's leadership to remain at arm's length; additionally, Barbara's thorough presentation allowed her to take some of the heat, answer all questions, and dispel rumors and fears. She acknowledged the lack of cooperation but said that because the wastewater issue was a joint problem, the two groups should approach the city together. This resulted in a tenuous agreement.

The golf club/village negotiating team appeared before the board of public utilities and said that as ratepayers they were very much in sympathy with the city's budget problems. However, they could not support plant closure and had been advised by their attorney that the contract could not be vacated. Nevertheless, they were very interested in working together to solve the problem.

Although the city attorney was fairly adamant and negative at the beginning, he became convinced that they should at least *try* to find a solution together. After all, it would be better for everyone if they could resolve the water and budget problems without resorting to an expensive legal fight.

The groups held a series of biweekly meetings during which they attempted to find a mutually satisfying solution. They had to work through some extremely complex technical, economic, and political issues that raised difficult questions. For example: How could they guarantee a continuing supply of water? How could they reduce the amount of water required and maintain the beautiful vegetation and scenery? How could they minimize the solution's cost? Who would be responsible for what costs? How could they obtain water during whatever building and transition phase was necessary? How could the various elected bodies keep from alienating significant blocs of voters?

As Barbara explained:

We had a kickoff meeting at the beginning of December with eight negotiation team members and the city attorney where I announced: "Everyone who lives in the community is a ratepayer of water, pays taxes, votes, so all have a stake . . . I prefer for the negotiating team to work in good faith, without any lawyers in the room. We want to work out a community level agreement which the attorneys can codify at the end. . . . That will save us all money." The city official wanted to work only with the golf course manager; he explained that he thought it would be "efficient to work with someone who knows the most about technology." I responded, "We all want efficiency, but we also need transparency; others might be happy to work that way, but I promise you that we will learn the technology if we need to and won't slow it down." And I insisted that we should all work together. He didn't like it; but we couldn't have subgroups. The club-village relationship was so fragile that any lack of trust would have made finding a solution impossible.

Gaining Credibility

The group began meetings by asking everyone to share what they wanted to know. They agreed that the group would build the needed data, run possible scenarios, and come up with a temporary agreement for the rest of the year, and a new agreement by July. Barbara described an early turning point in which she found a way to have even the sophisticated public utility commission members take her seriously:

We were asking how the city decided to create a master plan; the city responded that it was part of a huge master plan, with a sub-report about Oakmont. I said I wanted to read it. They responded, "No you don't; it's three inches thick." I replied, "I am going on some long flights. I can do the homework." I picked up the reports, and vowed to read them before the next scheduled meeting—the day after I finished a cruise.

I read and highlighted the reports during my trip, and indicated questions, and then took it in to our next negotiation meeting at 9 AM. The two city guys said, "We should probably look at the reports, so we can talk next time." I said, "No, I looked at it already, and I have some questions. On page 4, there is a reference to *nephelometric turbidity units (NTUs)*, and a set of requirements which were flunked. How? Why?" They didn't know. Sometimes you have to deal with experts who want to act like the smartest people in the room. If you want to play, you have to do the hard work in service of the goal—not just to show off. These men were floored that anyone had bothered to read that entire thick report. My efforts showed we were serious about joint decision making and contributing, and would take the time necessary to do it. One part of the report cited seven scenarios which the city employees claimed we couldn't analyze without a contract. I suggested we open all of the scenarios for now, along with any others, and urged, "Let's build a bunch of scenarios, and act as if we are unstuck." I think that helped them begin to loosen up and work together.

An Early Test

It wasn't always so easy to keep building trust. As Barbara reported:

We had said that we wanted to work with transparency and be really open with our own constituencies. Since individual golf club members had started writing letters to the editors of the local papers—and not necessarily well-informed ones—we knew that we needed to respond. We told the guys from the city I was putting together PowerPoint presentations for everyone, and that the president of the village association had written to the editor to give perspective. We gave them a copy and said we would call them if the paper decided to publish it. The problem was that the paper never told us that they had done so—and we woke up on Saturday morning to see it in print. The guys from the city were furious and put us through the ringer at the next meeting. We had taken a tough stance because the city attorney had been so hard line about "closing the plant now." We apologized, and promised to run all communications in both directions from that point on. We kept our promise, and gave them a chance to add whatever they wanted. That created a genuine sense of trust going forward.

Nearing Agreement, Internal Dissent from Unplanned-For Stakeholders

It took a great deal of work and increasing collaboration, but the groups kept their goals in mind. They were open about the cost differences in various schemes, agreed that they didn't want to use potable water on the golf course, and discovered that efficiency was a mutual criterion that appealed to both sides. Finally, the negotiations group narrowed on a creative and mutually satisfactory plan. However, they soon faced some unanticipated opposition.

A few members of the Oakmont planning and development committee (OPDC) had been extremely powerful in land and planning issues; however, they'd always worked totally behind the scenes. Barbara knew they existed but either had not realized or didn't want to face that they would be unhappy enough at being cut out of the process that they would try to undermine any agreement. At the last minute, two of them had gotten elected to the community board and insisted that they be put on the negotiations committee. Barbara feared that this would totally destroy the hard-won trust that they'd built. She consulted with other key golf club officers and the village association along with their lawyer. All agreed that they shouldn't involve the disgruntled OPDC members in the negotiations.

Despite her open and collaborative style, or perhaps because of it, Barbara was extremely uncomfortable at the idea of confronting two unhappy people who were used to getting their way. She spent a great deal of time first trying to get past her irritation at their "old boy" ways. They seemed to consider themselves above others and all the rules, so it was hard *not* to stereotype them. She found her hands shaking when preparing a negative note to them about joining the negotiations. Then she realized what she had to do to make things easier for both parties: figure out what their currencies were. She had to hone in on what they really cared about and how they could come out reasonably satisfied, or at least less *dis*satisfied. She imagined how important they must have felt being able to control things behind the scenes and how satisfied they must have been to have others perceive them as experts on complex land and development issues. She also appreciated the unscheduled time they probably had on their hands as longtime retirees. She decided that she had to be prepared to face them down. As such, she met with each of them individually, listened a lot, and eventually made a decision together that the village association board would not add any new members to the negotiating team. This worked well enough to avoid all-out warfare, and the process went on uninterrupted.

Barbara also let them know that the community was very positive about the work done and solution proposed, and that she wanted to work together going forward—if they were cooperative. She also hinted that she would hate to have to publish in the golf club's biweekly news column that all but a few self-interested factions were positive about the process. Fortunately, she didn't have to.

In the meantime, Barbara submitted an application for an opening on the OPDC board. She thought that she could serve to build bridges between the golf course and an important committee of the village association. She got quite a bit of support from key officials.

Saving Face for Elected Officials

Barbara also spent a great deal of time in one-on-one conversations with golf club and village officers, finding out what they needed, and trying to set things up so they could be successful. She was determined to be looking after everyone's benefit and not just golf club interests. She said repeatedly that the desired outcomes were a secure source of water on a continuing basis for the club, the sustained beautiful, open spaces with wildlife for the village, and reasonable water rates for the city.

Legal Hitches

A few new problems surfaced when it was time to turn the agreement over to the lawyers for official drafting. Because the city attorney didn't have time to do the first draft, he gave it to the golf club's attorney. But this version would have been very expensive for the city, so the city had a go. They drafted a version whose standard construction contract language called for an extremely expensive elaborate project management process. Both sides agreed that it was not what they wanted; but then they had to work out the question of liability for the construction and ultimate costs. Again, they worked collaboratively to determine how to reduce the risk on both sides, and were ultimately able to create a mutually satisfactory contract.

However, they still needed the interested parties' approval. The city people worried about signing a contract only with the golf club, in case the village association later claimed that they did not have to honor a contract of which they weren't part. Barbara and her colleagues then had to get the members of the Oakmont village association board to sign off. It became clear to Barbara that she'd need to hold individual meetings with each board member, and she proceeded to make the rounds. Having to sell a good solution one-on-one was new to her; she had been so focused on the complexities of inventing a satisfactory solution that she had not thought much about gaining ultimate approval. She started with the current president, but brought along the member of the negotiating team who was the former president to help. Although she eventually got everyone on board, she was amazed by the individual variations in what board members cared about. She had to listen carefully for each person's currencies and frame the arguments accordingly. She also discovered that in some cases, it was important to identify members who influenced other members and get them to work on the recalcitrant ones. It was a process of influencing the influencers. The ultimate collaborative solution was finally passed by the City Council by a 7-0 vote.

The entire experience helped Barbara sort her priorities and identify her ultimate aspiration: to bring simplified versions of existing health care technology to underserved populations. She also learned a lot about what it might take to start such an organization. She got in touch with and practiced her ability to face up to negative responses, despite her preference to be positive all the time. Ultimately, she also learned a lot about owning her own behavior—what she came to call "leading from the front" instead of merely facilitating others' initiatives.

Lessons for Influencing on a Grand Scale

Here are some of the takeaways from Barbara Spangler's arduous efforts to induce many parties with diverse interests and high potential for battling rather than problem solving to collaborate. The lessons apply to similar multiparty situations you may face.

- **Once you have a vision of your overall goal, stick with it.** Barbara and her allies gained confidence that they would come to a mutually acceptable solution, even though they weren't exactly sure how. However, they were committed to figuring out what the right thing to do was, and then getting the various constituencies to adopt it. It helps to be good at, or mobilize others to help create, feasible mutually satisfactory solutions. Don't leap to the first possible solution; create multiple options for consideration and revision.

- **Identify stakeholders early.** When presented as part of a model, the need to identify relevant stakeholders seems self-evident; however, it can be hard to do this up front in complex situations. This instance showed how failure to do so can interject unexpected roadblocks at inconvenient times. Fortunately, Barbara was able to work her way around each of these roadblocks.

- **Do your homework.** Good intentions don't go far if you are not credible with powerful knowledgeable people.

    Even in the unlikeliest of circumstances, start with a partnership mind-set, and don't give up too fast when others do not readily welcome it. There were plenty of people on all sides of the wastewater plant issues who assumed that other parties would be intransigent and that they needed to be belligerent from the beginning. This kind of preemptive attack is so common that many people simply assume there is no other way to function. There are plenty of instances when even the best-intentioned partnerlike approaches do not work; however, there's no chance they'll work if you don't give them a try! It's better to point out the negative consequences at the first resistance and try again than to just give up.

- **Once engaged with the key players, work to get the team committed to each other and to the outcome.** Although it sounds individually driven, Barbara points out that she definitely didn't accomplish this without drawing on the entire negotiating group's skills, talents, and insights.

- **Keep in mind that a wide range of responses is likely with multiple players.** This may seem obvious. However, it can be hard to remember when you're trying to make something happen that others may see things very differently—and value different aspects of the situation. Even individuals on the same side of an issue can agree on overall goals but have very different ideas about how to achieve them. Some currencies will apply to a group; others will be individual.

- **Keep thinking win-win, but be ready for some asymmetry.** It isn't always possible for everyone to get everything they are interested in, though it is a useful starting point. Don't let idealism and perfection be the enemy of the satisfactory.

- **Demonstrate a constant willingness to listen—even when you and others don't agree.** Opponents often have enough reason to disagree, but it isn't a good idea to add to their irritation. This can be difficult when you have very strong feelings about the outcomes, but you must practice self-discipline. Besides, sometimes you learn important things when you listen—contingencies you hadn't realized, or even that you are (gulp!) wrong.

- **You can't be afraid of negative reactions—or, for that matter, of being warm and supportive.** Expand your own range of emotions and tolerance for diverse reactions. Consider whether you have an unlimited need to be liked; it usually means that you are ceding control of your behavior to others and their reactions.

We have said from the outset that influencing powerful people requires finding out what they care about and finding ways to give some of it in return for what you need. Putting that into practice requires a considerable amount of hard-nosed analysis, sometimes up close and sometimes at a great distance—and if you gain access, both. But it almost always comes down to you and your values, goals, and emotions, which are inevitably part of the process. Not only is some intuition usually required to tune in, but so is a large helping of courage to allow you to act on what you come to see as necessary for impact. This isn't easy when the much higher-powered person or group can respond in negative ways, such as with anger, indifference, or retaliation. Yet powerful people do get influenced, helping not only the influencers but also themselves. We hope you find the courage to use what you have learned to make the difference you desire.

Additional Resources

Training Programs

1. Babson College offers a residential five-day executive development program, *Leadership and Influence*, exploring vision, teamwork and other leadership competencies needed to influence at all levels of an organization. This highly experiential program is for managers who have direct reports managing others, and combines videos, case discussions, role plays, simulations, and a day of leadership problem-solving activities linked to *Influence without Authority* and post-heroic concepts. Participants request confidential questionnaire feedback on leadership style from peers and direct reports, and utilize the results at the program. With a faculty team led by Allan Cohen, the program has also been customized for numerous companies. More information is available from Babson Executive Education, Babson Park, MA 02157-0310, Phone: 781-239-4354 or Toll-Free Phone: 800-882-EXEC, or http://www.babson.edu/bee. E-mail: exec@babson.edu.

2. Stanford Graduate School of Business offers a residential five-day *Executive Program in Leadership: The Effective Use of Power*, designed to help experienced managers put effective, collaborative methods of leadership to work for their organizations. Participants will discover how to develop and maintain vision and power by tapping into their team's valuable leadership potential and will gain hands-on experience through videos, case discussions, role

231

plays, and simulations, linked to *Influence without Authority* and post-heroic concepts. Participants request confidential questionnaire feedback on leadership style from peers and direct reports, and utilize the results at the program. With a faculty team led by David Bradford, the program runs in the summer and has also been customized for numerous companies. More information is available from Stanford Executive Education, 655 Knight Way, Stanford, CA 94305-5015, http://www.gsb.stanford.edu/exed/lead/. Phone: 650-723-3341 or Toll-Free Phone: 866-542-2205.

3. An online program, *Resolving Interpersonal Issues*, a program for dealing with difficult relationships based on concepts from *Influence without Authority* is available from PDI Ninth House, http://www.pdinh.com/sites/default/files/u20/ResolvingInter personalIssues.pdf.

4. Custom training by Allan Cohen, David Bradford, or several associates has been designed for half-day, one-day, and two-day programs. These can stand alone or be integrated into longer executive development programs. Contacts: cohen@babson.edu or bradford_david@gsb.stanford.edu.

Speeches

Keynote speeches, inspirational or informational talks on influence, and various applications are available from Allan Cohen or David Bradford. Contacts as above.

Survey

A 360-degree instrument on influence, or on influence and leadership, tied to the concepts in *Influence without Authority* and/or our leadership book, *Power Up*, is available. The questions ask colleagues, subordinates, and boss(es) how the person is doing now, and how the respondent would prefer the person to behave. All questions are tied to actions that can be changed, so that the results are practical and connected to what people want. Sample questions are available at http://influencewithoutauthority.com.

Cases on Influence

Extended examples and analyses of people who have exercised or need to exercise influence are available at the website at http://influence withoutauthority.com.

Notes

Chapter 2   How Power Differentials Blind Smart People

1. P.G. Zimbardo, C. Maslach, and C. Haney, "Reflections on the Stanford Prison Experiment: Genesis, Transformation, Consequences," in *Obedience to Authority: Current Perspectives on the Milgram Paradigm*, ed. T. Blass (Mahwah, NJ: Erlbaum, 1999), 193–237; Barry Oshry, *Leading Systems: Lessons from the Power Lab* (San Francisco: Berrett-Koehler, 1999); Lee Bolman and Terry Deal, "A Simple—But Powerful—Power Simulation," *Exchange: The Organizational Behavior Teaching Journal* 4, no. 3 (1979): 38–42.

2. Vicki Haddock, "Psychology of Power: What Drives This Powerful Men? And Where Are They Driving Us?" http://compenetration.word press.com/2008/06/09/psychology-of-power-what-drives-this-power ful-men-and-where-are-they-driving-us.

3. G. Chen, L.K. Trevino, and D.C. Hambrick, "CEO Elitist Association: A New Understanding of an Executive Behavioral Pattern," *The Leadership Quarterly* 20 (2009): 316–328; J. Lammers and D. Stapel, "Power Increases Dehumanization," *Group Processes and Intergroup Relations* 14 (2011): 113.

4. Cameron Anderson and Jennifer Berdahl, "Experience of Power: Examining the Effects of Power on Approach and Inhibition Tendencies," *Journal of Personality and Social Psychology* 83, no. 6 (2002): 1362–1377; J.L. Berdahl and P. Martorana, "Effects of Power on Emotion and Expression during a Controversial Group Discussion," *European Journal of Social Psychology: Special Issue on Social Power* 36 (2006): 497–510; A.D. Galinsky, J.C. Magee, D.H. Gruenfeld, J. Whitson, and K. Liljenquist, "Power Reduces the Press of the Situation: Implications for Creativity,

Conformity, and Dissonance," *Journal of Personality and Social Psychology* 95, no. 6 (2008): 1450–1466.

5. A. Guinote, "Power and Goal Pursuit," Study 4, *Personality and Social Psychology Bulletin* 33 (2007): 1076–1087.

6. A.A. Eaton, P.S. Visser, J.A. Krosnick, and S. Anand, "Social Power and Attitude Strength over the Life Course," *Personality and Social Psychology Bulletin* 35 (2009): 1646–1660.

7. P. Briñol, R.E. Petty, C. Valle, D.D. Rucker, and A. Becerra, "The Effects of Message Recipients' Power before and after Persuasion: A Self-Validation Analysis," *Journal of Personality and Social Psychology* 93 (2007): 1040–1053.

8. Chen, Trevino, and Hambrick, "CEO Elitist Association: A New Understanding of an Executive Behavioral Pattern," 316–328.

9. Jennifer R. Overbeck and Bernadette Park, "Powerful Perceivers, Powerless Objects: Flexibility of Powerholders' Social Attention," *Organizational Behavior and Human Decision Processes* 99, no. 2 (March 2006): 227–243.

10. Roderick M. Kramer, "The Harder They Fall," *Harvard Business Review OnPoint Edition* (October 2003).

11. Joris Lammers et al., "Power Increases Hypocrisy: Moralizing in Reasoning, Immorality in Behavior," *Psychological Science* 21 (2010): 737. doi:10.1177/1948550611418679.

12. Dana Carney, "Defend Your Research: Powerful People are Better Liars," *Harvard Business Review* (May 2010).

13. Adam D. Galinsky, Joe C. Magee, M. Ena Inesi, and Deborah H. Gruenfeld, "Power and Perspectives Not Taken," *Psychological Science* 17, no. 12 (2006): 1068–1073.

14. The woeful saga of Jeff Kindler and all the subsequent quotes about it come from Peter Elkind and Jennifer Reingold, with Doris Burke, "Inside Pfizer's Palace Coup," *Fortune* (August 15, 2011): 164, 3, 76- XX.

15. David C. McClelland and David H. Burnham, "Power Is the Great Motivator," *Harvard Business Review* (January 1, 2003).

16. Savita Bhave, *Casting a Destiny: The Biography of Chandran Menon*, trans. Nandu Dange (Pune: Ameya Books, 2004), 43–44; Allan R. Cohen, "Training for the Transition from Entrepreneur to Manager: A Case Study," in *Administrative Issues in Developing Economies*, ed. K. Rothwell (Lexington, MA: D.C. Heath, 1970).

Chapter 3 How Power Differentials Give Smart People Laryngitis

1. Amy Edmonson and James Detert, HBS interview and working paper, 2011, discussing J. R. Detert and Amy C. Edmondson, "Implicit Voice Theories: Taken-for-Granted Rules of Self-Censorship at Work," *Academy of Management Journal* 54, no. 3 (June 2011).

2. Ithai Stern and James D. Westphal, "Stealthy Footsteps to the Boardroom: Executives' Backgrounds, Sophisticated Interpersonal Influence Behavior, and Board Appointments," *Administrative Science Quarterly* 55, no. 2 (2010): 278–319.

Chapter 7 Building a Partnership Relationship with Your Boss

1. In our previous books, *Managing for Excellence* (1984) and *Power Up: Transforming Organizations through Shared Leadership* (1998), we called this prevalent but outmoded overresponsibility the heroic mind-set.

Chapter 8 The Art—and Responsibility—of Helping Your Boss Succeed

1. Again, heroic leadership and its antidotes, post-heroic or shared responsibility leadership, are the themes of our books, *Managing for Excellence* and *Power Up*.

Chapter 10 Framing Your Change Strategy

1. Personal interview with Allan Cohen, September 2011. Used with permission.

2. This list was developed by Liam Fahey, a strategy consultant, whose ideas have helped shape ours.

3. See "Monica Ashley" case, Cohen and Bradford, www.influencewithout authority.com.

4. This now widely adopted model was originally developed by George M. Beal, Everett M. Rogers, and Joe M. Bohlen, "Validity of the Concept of Stages in the Adoption Process," *Rural Sociology* 22, no. 2 (1957): 166–168.

5. All of her comments were made to Allan in interviews and appeared in his article "CMOs and Influence," *The Chief Marketing Officer Journal* (February 2009).

Chapter 11 What Do the Powerful Care About?

1. From author interview reported in Allan R. Cohen, "CMOs and Influence," *The Chief Marketing Officer Journal* (February 2009).

Chapter 12 Action Steps for Gaining Access to Powerful People

1. Scott Kirsner, "Collision Course: Toyota Creates the Ultimate SneakerNet," *Fast Company* (January/February 2000). These comments were supplemented in a personal interview with Dames and Allan Cohen on September 22, 2011.

2. The movie is based on the memoir *Hard Sell* by Jamie Reidy.

3. The clever blog was by Christine Comaford, "I Stalked Steve Jobs (And How to Get a Meeting with ANY VIP)," *Forbes* (November 10, 2011).

4. We are grateful to Babson colleague Bala Iyer for his insights in this new territory of social media and reputation.

5. Leslie Kwoh, "Reverse Mentoring Cracks Workplace," *Wall Street Journal* (November 28, 2011), B7.

Chapter 14 The Contours of Change

1. Liz Kowalczyk, "A Dream Realized, and Lives Reborn: With Drive, Diplomacy, and Heart, a Young Surgeon Made Boston a Face-Transplant Leader," *Boston Globe* (October 2, 2011).

Index